ASINAMALI

ASINAMALI:

University Struggles in Post-Apartheid South Africa

Edited by

Richard Pithouse

Africa World Press, Inc.

P.O. Box 1892
Trenton, NJ 08607

P.O. Box 48
Asmara, ERITREA

Africa World Press, Inc.

P.O. Box 1892
Trenton, NJ 08607

P.O. Box 48
Asmara, ERITREA

Copyright ©2006 Africa World Press

First Printing 2006

Book Design: James Lindenschmidt
Cover Design: Dapo Ojo-Ade

Library of Congress Cataloging-in-Publication Data

Asinamali : university struggles in post-apartheid South Africa / edited
by Richard Pithouse.
    p. cm.
  Includes bibliographical references and index.
  ISBN 1-59221-435-5 (hard cover) -- ISBN 1-59221-436-3 (pbk.)
  1. Education, Higher--South Africa. 2. Discrimination in higher
education--South Africa. 3. Universities and colleges--South Africa.
I. Pithouse, Richard, 1970- .
LA1538.A85 2006
378.68--dc22

                              20050276

This book is dedicated to Michael Makhabane who was murdered by the public order policing unit during a peaceful protest against the exclusion of poor students from the University of Durban-Westville on May 16, 2000.

Contents

Preface and Acknowledgments

Editors of the Committee for Academic
Freedom in Africa Newsletter

Asinamali examines the struggles waged by students and teachers against structural adjustment in post-apartheid South African universities. Written by scholar/activists in South Africa, *Asinamali* is an important contribution to our understanding of both social struggle in contemporary Africa and the impact of adjustment and the neo-liberal agenda on African higher education.

By cooperating in its publication, the Committee for Academic Freedom in Africa (CAFA) continues the task which motivated the formation of our organization in 1991 and which we have carried out since: (1) analyzing the root causes and the socio-political implications of the neo-liberal attack on public education in Africa, (2) documenting the effects of "adjustment" on African universities as well as the resistance of students, teachers and other staff to the imposition of this program and, most important, (3) building networks of solidarity between academics and students in North America and their African colleagues.

In presenting this book to the public we want to thank CAFA's sponsors and supporters for their help over the years. We also want to thank all those who have made this book possible. First and foremost, we thank Richard Pithouse, the editor of *Asinamali*, and the South African colleagues who contributed to making this book a unique contribution to our understanding of the struggles of students and teachers in post-apartheid South Africa. We also want to thank Andrew Nash for his editorial work on the manuscript. We also extend special thanks to Kassahun Checole of Africa World Press and to Dennis Brutus for the support they have given to this project and the concerned advice have given CAFA's work over many years of collaboration. Their commitment to the liberation struggle in Africa has been a constant inspiration for our work.

Foreword

Dennis Brutus

Students, black and white, have always played an important role in political activism in South Africa. Their political presence in the life of academia dates back at least to 1948, when the National Party government came to power. Segregation had always existed in South Africa, but it was intensified under the apartheid doctrine, and the passing of a number of laws including the Extension of University Education Act, which institutionalized apartheid in higher education. The apartheid doctrine defined the position of each "race" in society. Whites were destined to a "dominant" position. Blacks and other non-white races were destined to a "subordinate" position. Blacks were also declared "not fit for labor above certain levels in society." It was stated that "they should not aspire to the green fields that were reserved for others."

From 1948 onwards, students mounted a continuous opposition against apartheid and Fort Hare students played a key role in it. The college was predominantly black, but it did not exclude whites and it also included coloreds and Asians. There were several political strands among the students. The strongest was African nationalism, as many students came from families who had experienced the colonial conquest wars and engaged in resistance, particularly in what were called Frontiers Wars or Kaffir Wars.

Fort Hare itself had been a military base in the frontier wars and close to it was a hillock, Sandile's Kop, that had been the base for resistance led by Xhosa Chiefs. The fort was used by the British Army in the Frontier Wars against the Africans.

Subsequently, it was taken over by the churches and turned into a college—Fort Hare University College at the time I was there—and, later, Fort Hare University. It was an ecumenical enterprise in which four churches were involved: Anglican/Episcopelian, Methodist, and Presbyterian. I was a student at the Anglican Dormitory called Beda College.

Another political strand centered on the struggle for land and the preservation of traditional values and customs. Land was a prominent issue in the consciousness of many Africans students who saw themselves and their parents being expropriated from their land; it was also a dominant issue for the African National Congress first formed in 1912, after the formation of the Union of South Africa in 1910. A third political strand was that of left-Marxist students, belonging to the South African Communist Party or the Fourth International, which brought Trotskyist and Stalinist influences within the movement. Later there would also be a Maoist influence. Inevitably there were strong petty bourgeois aspirations as well among the students.

Meanwhile, white students too were protesting—at the University of Cape Town, Natal University, and at Witwatersrand University in Johannesburg—as liberal South Africans saw the new segregationist laws as an attack on academic freedom and as attempts by Afrikaans to impose their control on the English liberal traditions. Thus, already in the 1940s, a student movement emerged that was mostly white, but included black students. It was called the National Union of South African Students (NUSAS). Although many black students, who took a more radical position, were critical of NUSAS, this organization served a useful purpose boosting the mobilization against apartheid. Among the predominantly white students' organizations, it also important to remember the African Resistance Movement (ARM) which, in the 1960s, specialized in sabotage actions against the apartheid regime. Often forgotten in the histories of the anti-apartheid struggle, the ARM was a very significant element in the anti-apartheid struggle, at one point sabotaging the entire electrical grid of Johannesburg, and bringing to a halt all of the town's factories.

Protests of various kinds were continuous; but they became especially marked with the proclamation of the Freedom Charter in 1955, that was adopted at a Congress of the People called by the African National Congress. 1955 was also the year when a new apartheid constitution was adopted, increasing racial restrictions. In response to it, a National Convention Movement was organized demanding a broader representation for all.

Starting with 1955, the demands of the students were those articulated in the Freedom Charter and the Ten Point Program of 1943: free education, the vote, jobs for all, a living wage, and the right to organize, which was especially important at a time when the government was attacking trade union activities. Student activism in South Africa peaked in the 1970s, when black students, largely inspired by Steven Biko and the Black Consciousness Movement, formed a more radical organization: the South African Student Organization (SASO).

Steven Biko was murdered in September 1977 by the South African security police after being interrogated at their headquarters in Port Elizabeth; but he was the inspiration for much of the student activism of the 1970s and after. This was particularly true of the massive student protest of 1976, that took place when the police killed hundred of high-school students during the Soweto uprising. The protest gave a powerful impulse to the resistance against apartheid all over the country at a time the African National Congress (ANC) and Pan African Congress (PAC) could not openly lead the movement having been banned since 1960, after the massacre at Sharpeville.

The most important development after the Soweto uprising was the creation of the United Democratic Front (UDF), a coalition of trade union, and civic organizations—churches, students, and other groups—that mounted the main challenge to the apartheid regime. In the end, the students became part of this much broader anti-apartheid movement, but they had consistently contributed to its development.

This movement, coming from all sectors of the population and from a wide variety of political positions, was probably the decisive internal factor in forcing the apartheid government to begin negotiations leading to the termination of apartheid. An especially important aspect of the movement's struggle were labor actions, including strikes, stay-at-home, and other forms of civil disobedience. At the same time, there were pressures from the armed resistance as well as the international divestment movement and international boycotts. The outcome was a transitional phase culminating with the Codesa talks where a new constitution was discussed and a Government of National Unity was set up.

The essays in *Asinamali* take up the story from here. They tell of a new phase of students' and teachers' activism directed against the structural adjustment of South African universities in line with the neoliberal GEAR program the ANC promulgated in 1996. This book is an important contribution that introduces people inside and outside South Africa to the courageous struggles that that are taking place in the schools of post-apartheid South Africa for the most important academic freedom: the right to study.

Introduction

by Richard Pithouse

> Each generation must out of relative obscurity discover its
> mission, fulfill it or betray it.
> —Frantz Fanon, *The Wretched of the Earth*

The afternoon of September 9, 2004 was cold and grey in
Durban. It didn't feel like spring. Outside the provincial Minister
of Education's offices two hundred or so students where
shivering under the banner of the Socialist Student Movement
singing *Asinamali* (We have no money) and demanding that poor
students not be excluded from universities and schools because
of an inability to pay fees. The Minister emerged through the
heavy gates to stand behind a row of riot police from the same
unit that had killed a student, Michael Makhabane, during a
protest against exclusions in Durban four years earlier. Amongst
the protestors' banners was one that read "Hector Petersen
Martyr of the Struggle Against Apartheid Education—Soweto
1976 * Michael Makhabane Martyr of the Struggle Against
Neoliberal Education—Durban 2000". It was pushed up right in
front of her. The Minister told the students that it was "a real
pity that Hector Petersen died in the struggle against Bantu
Education". She said nothing at all about Makhabane but put her
fist up and shouted *Amandla!* (Power!), the ANC slogan. Ashwin
Desai, fired from the campus where Makhabane was killed for
opposing initial shifts to neoliberalism four years before the
murder, grabbed the microphone in fury and spat his rage at her
hypocrisy. For a moment the power began to shift as students

shouted back with their own pain and anger. But when the protest was over the minister went back behind her gates and into her building and the students huddled in the first drops of the coming rain still singing *Asinamali*. It was another ordinary day in the relentlessly steady defeat of much that was won by South African students in their struggles against apartheid education.[1]

Regular readers of the Committee for Academic Freedom in Africa (CAFA.) *Newsletter* will be well aware that during the 1990s neoliberal policies, often under the direct supervision of the World Bank and IMF, sought to cut state spending on higher education by down grading, merging and closing African Universities and shifting the cost of education from the state to students and their families.[2] This process, together with the fact that the World Bank was openly arguing that Universities were an unaffordable luxury for African states, led many to conclude that the dramatic increase in university enrollment during the 1960s and 1970s (enrollment levels that had been close to zero during the colonial period rose to 1 percent by 1980) would be largely or even completely reversed.[3] But as CAFA noted:

> This, however, did not happen in the 1990s. African students systematically and aggressively rejected the World Bank's higher education financial policies as an attack on Africa's collective future. In demonstration after demonstration the students' major demand has been to preserve and increase access to university education in the face of the World Bank's will to "shut them down."[4]

Despite often violent state repression, student activism successfully halted the decline in university enrollment. But it was not able to challenge the major decrease in investment in university education that led to a dramatic collapse of infrastructure, retrenchments, an increase in authoritarianism by university managers and the state, a general decline in working conditions, and a calamitous loss of good students, teachers, and researchers, to the West. CAFA declared a stalemate.

Recent statements from the Bank indicate a shift from the view that African universities are an unaffordable luxury to the view that they have an important role to play in "development."[5] This is best understood as part of a broader shift by the Bank towards a rhetorical commitment to participation and empowerment[6] and a practical commitment to seek more effective ways of implementing its central policy prescriptions by abandoning its demand for a minimalist state in favor of a demand for 'effective bureaucracies and activist states in the implementation of structural adjustment programmes'.[7] The rhetorical commitment to participation and empowerment matches the shift in U.S. foreign policy, consequent to popular struggles, away from creating and supporting overtly authoritarian regimes and towards supporting formally democratic governments and "civil society organizations" that are loyal to the substantively anti-democractic neoliberal project.[8] It provides much of the legitimation for the Bank's attempts to generate local capacity to advance and to mask (and to advance by masking) its agenda.

These projects are not undertaken in isolation. The Bank's policy of "harmonizing" and seeking further "coherence" between its policies and those of the IMF, the WTO and certain donors[9] (most notoriously USAID) means that there are large amounts of donor funding and NGO support available for academics, departments, institutions and projects within the African academy that function, under the guise of "partnership" to advance the neoliberal project. This has produced a situation where there are very well resourced nodes of compradorism within an academy that remains in deep structural crisis. These nodes of compradorism serve to gather information for the social forces that fund them and to legitimate the agenda of these forces by giving it an appearance of indigeneity and academic integrity. They are also predatory on the broader academy. They often exploit public resources, including many of the people who have been able to emerge from the crisis ridden public university system with good skills, without investing in the general university system. A typical example of this would be a small donor-funded research institute that removes talented academics from the general teaching and research of a university and directs them to work on donor-directed projects. Furthermore these nodes of well-funded compradorism also allow university managers, states, and donors to claim that African universities are flourishing while their actual ability to teach undergraduate students and conduct independent research is collapsing. Of course this is not to suggest that all donor-funded projects are necessarily neoliberal in orientation but that fact does not mean that the problems outlined above are not pervasive.

Not all the failures of post-colonial African universities can be blamed on the Bank or the authoritarian regimes and national elites often propped up by U.S. and Soviet imperialism. In 1992

Mahmood Mamdani, speaking with reference to the broader African post-colonial experience, warned South Africans that post-colonial policies with an "accent on affirmative action ('Africanization') and not democratization, tended to strengthen and legitimate colonial institutions and practices by removing them from the racial stigma of [the past]."[10] And, indeed, as Fanon famously argued, a culpable laziness can lead intellectuals to buy into the idea that progress should be reduced to the deracialization of domination.

Writing within the broad context of the current situation Adebayo Olukoshi and Paul Tiyambe Zeleza introduce their recent edited collection of essays on *African Universities in the Twenty-First Century* by noting that:

> The context and content of the challenge of redefining the university and securing its place of course differ between countries, but they all reflect the decomposition of the old social contract between the university, the state, and society in which higher education was valued as a public and intellectual good which, moreover, dovetailed into visions of nation-building and national development. As market imperatives and ideology have gained or are struggling to gain supremacy universities are increasingly valorised or find themselves compelled to seek valorisation for their private and vocational good.[11]

This shift is a universal phenomenon and the results for public universities in South Africa are very similar, in kind if not always in degree, to the results elsewhere in the continent and the world.[12] Cost-recovery policies result in fee prices that exclude poor students and make it very difficult for many families to think of education as anything other than an economic investment with consequent pressures on students to orient their study and practice towards corporate, state and donor power. Simultaneously the provision of food, accommodation and reading materials is commodified exerting further exclusionary pressure on poor students and making life extremely difficult for many students who are only able to mobilize enough money to win access. This in turn places poor students in the system under tremendous material and psychological pressures. In a number of instances these pressures have manifested themselves in highly gendered ways. For example, poor female students sometimes provide sex and housekeeping for richer male students in exchange for financial support. The emergence of highly reactionary and deeply gendered religious and cultural discourses and practices is also becoming more common as are various forms of xenophobia and homophobia. Moreover universities are increasingly physically separated from the broader society in the manner of business parks and poor people often face severe surveillance and harassment if they succeed in entering campuses at all.

Curricula are increasingly directed away from critique and a respectful engagement with the lived experience of ordinary people and towards the perceived needs of the market and the requirements of the institutions that organize the market. Often departments and courses that are not profitable - especially in the arts and humanities are summarily shut down. Similarly the general commodification of research means that universities increasingly become service providers to corporate interests, the World Bank, donors and the state. Academics often become consultants rather than intellectuals and are increasingly (in practice, if not always in principle) assessed on their ability to raise funds rather than the quality of their research and teaching. Talented academics are often removed from undergraduate teaching altogether and post-graduate students are routinely expected to work on funded projects rather than to pursue independent inquiry. Many academics who do not go the consultancy route find themselves unable to survive on meager salaries and have to take on other work. Junior staff members are frequently severely exploited in terms of working hours, the allocation of credit for work done and low rates of pay. Collegial governance is replaced with corporate modes of authoritarianism. Workers are retrenched and their jobs outsourced. The language of "excellence" and claims about aspirations to be "world class" are used to legitimate a wholesale abandonment of critique in favor of commodification. This is a very familiar story in Africa and around the world.

However, there are two key differences between the current situation in South Africa and the rest of the continent. The first is due to the fact that structural adjustment only came to South Africa in 1996. There had been World Bank directed shifts towards neoliberal policies under the Botha regime[13] but the apartheid state lacked the political credibility to be able to implement a full scale structural adjustment program.[14] However the African National Congress used its political legitimacy to take up a structural adjustment program with enthusiasm.[15] The second key difference between the South African situation and that of the rest of the continent is that independence came to

South Africa even later, relatively speaking, than structural adjustment and in the context of a settlement with a large and powerful settler descended population. The fact that a compromised democracy arrived in 1994 and structural adjustment in 1996 allowed the ANC to use both the failures and successes of the former as cover to legitimate the latter.

The ANC has sought to reduce struggles against racism to the deracialization of privilege and this project has been combined with the development of neoliberal policies that entrench relations of exclusion and domination.[16] The deracialization of the elite sphere and the implementation of neoliberal policies that further privilege that sphere against the rest of society are combined in a project called "transformation" which is presented as anti-racist and in the interests of national development.

In the higher education system this has produced a massive restructuring of the university system that will see the reduction of the number of universities from 36 to 21. This restructuring is presented as a project aimed at racial equity as it will do away with many of the historically racialized institutions created under colonialism and apartheid. However, Jonathan Jansen offers convincing empirical evidence to support his argument that "None of the mergers underway suggest that greater equity has been achieved in terms of either students or staffing. That is, none of the mergers either intended, or achieved, greater representation of black and women students in the new institution."[17] It seems clear that the mergers are in fact a typical neoliberal cost cutting exercise[18] that will result in an as yet unknown reduction in the number of staff and students in the higher education system. Early indications are very worrying. In late August 2004 the Department of Education informed the Parliament's education portfolio committee that across the board reductions in student numbers are expected within the next three years.[19] Fazel Khan's explanation of what the cuts will mean for the newly merged University of KwaZulu-Natal is worth citing at some length:

> The mandarins at the Department of Education (DoE) argued that the merger that created the new University of KwaZulu-Natal (UKZN) in 2004 was a transformatory project aimed at undoing the apartheid legacy in higher education. But just months into the existence of the new institution the future is looking very bleak for poor students hoping to enter UKZN. According to the "Student

Enrollment and Planning 2005 to 2007" document recently proposed by the DoE to the UKZN management, total student enrollment is to be cut from 43,000 to 34,000 by 2007. As a result, UKZN, legitimated in part by claims that it would provide greater access to students from disadvantaged communities, is to reduce its new student intake.

Of course neoliberalism's scythe will fall most heavily on the poor—people who lack resources as a direct result of a history of racialized conquest, domination, exploitation and marginalization. From the beginning of 2005 first year students are to be limited to 6,500 across the all campuses as compared to 7,633 that were enrolled last year. This means a cut in real terms of 2,366, if one takes into consideration the projected increase to 8,566 first year students. Since there are close to 20,000 first year applications annually, a system has to be used to weed out unsuitable applicants. With the proposed cut in first time enrollment, the one feasible criterion would be to raise the entry-points requirement into the institution. This will penalize learners from indigent communities where 83 percent of schools have no libraries or textbooks, teachers are often poorly qualified, and students walk long distances to school and often arrive hungry. Instead, the already privileged students from private schools with state of the art libraries and computer classes will benefit. Furthermore these students can afford a university education—much to the delight of those in the DoE who conform to neoliberalism's foundational principle, cost-recovery, and cry "sustainability". In such circumstances it is no stretch to believe that the university will ensure that those who can afford to pay for tuition would constitute the greater majority of qualifying students. Already this year's registration fees have increased by R2,000 for students from the former Westville campus where fees were, as a direct result of years of struggle, lower than the former Natal campus.[20]

There are clear tensions between the projects to deracialize the University system and to reorganize it along neoliberal lines. The most obvious of these tensions is that the commodification of education clearly serves the interests of elites and class is highly racialized in South Africa. But there is an additional tension in that the racialization of South African universities under apartheid was not just about access to institutions and the division of labor within them. It was also about a range of other things such as which languages were seen as able to carry academic work and which languages were only fit for anthropological study; which social forces in society were seen as carrying transformative energies; what was naturalized and what was historicized and in who's interests; where reason was located and so on. Deracializing the division of labor (who does) is not the same as deracializing the nature of the labor (what is done). On the contrary deracializing the former can legitimize the increasing racism of the latter. Marx's observation that "The more a dominant class is able to absorb the best people from the dominated classes, the more solid and dangerous is its rule"[21] has powerful resonance in contemporary South Africa.

In fact, the World Bank and its associated donor agencies that exert such a powerful impact on the parts of the South African academy that can be connected to "development" (an expanding category—history can become "heritage" and then "tourism," etc.), that speak a language delinked from the classic racial stereotypes (laziness, dirtiness, dangerous men and willing women, etc., etc.) that legitimated colonial domination from race, and projects them onto the global poor of all races in order to legitimate contemporary forms of domination that entrench inequalities previously created in explicitly racist terms.[22]

Moreover the Bank's gaze is locked into the present. With neoliberalism we are always at the beginning of year zero. And without history poverty is naturalized as is, by implication, wealth. Under colonialism, "The cause is the consequence; you are rich because you are white, you are white because you are rich."[23] Under neoliberalism the cause is still the consequence: you are poor because you are The Poor; you are The Poor because you are poor. In South Africa the political amnesia that this produces is, although in different forms, equally useful for the old white elite and the rising black elite. The white elite relentlessly seeks to naturalize its privilege by disguising its history of conquest, expropriation and exploitation and presents itself as the modernizing vanguard while the black elite seeks, with equal vigor, to entrench a systemic forgetting of the radical values of the struggles that bought it to power to be able to claim to be the vanguard of a project called "transformation." In both cases the majority, who are becoming steadily poorer, are told that everything depends on nurturing and perpetuating the privilege of a minority who are becoming steadily richer.

Furthermore this is compounded by the fact that claims about the instant success of deracialization are often articulated in the language of the crude and essentializing multiculturalism more generally associated with the tourist industry's willingness to play to stereotypes. So, for example, many universities have new logos, slogans and posters that reference highly racialized popular western ideas of Africa while the actual content of their work has, to a significant degree, only changed since apartheid in so far as it has accommodated itself to the neoliberal agenda.

The general thrust towards a co-opted academy that looks towards dominant donor funded ideologies (rather than the rich legacies of the struggles against apartheid and contemporary struggles against neoliberalism) is well captured by the fact that in the same week that the United Nations human development report indicated that South Africa's human development index had steadily declined since 1995 and had now slid back to 1975 levels, leaving South Africa ranked below occupied Palestine and Equatorial Guinea,[24] the South African Association for Political Science (SAAPS) issued an invitation to its biennial conference that began as follows: "Following South Africa's successful first decade of freedom, it is important that scholars and the business community come together and examine the achievements of the decade."[25]

The evident contradiction between the celebratory discourse of SAAPS, with its uncritical, even celebratory, investment in "partnership," and the reality of deepening social crisis illuminates a central failure of the bulk of the post-apartheid academy. Evidence for the existence of the social crisis is readily available—even the government's own statistics agency concedes that, in real terms, average black African household income declined 19 percent from 1995 to 2000 while white household income was up 15 percent.[26] But the bulk of the academy is deeply invested in dominant discourses which seek to achieve the simultaneous commodification and deracialization of the elite sphere. For some people this investment may be purely ideological but for many it is very clearly material. A considerable number of academics have become very rich over the last ten years. Many do not consider writing an article without "a budget" and take great care not to offend the powerful. When the Vice-Chancellor of UKZN wrote an outrageous and ill informed article in the national newspaper *This Day* celebrating Margaret Thatcher's "reforms" of the British university system as an example to be followed, not one UKZN academic responded.

Of course, some critical spaces are being produced and sustained by sheer commitment. But they are extracting a high price from the few individuals who take the risks and put in the extra hours to nurture and defend the idea of critique and the intellectual vocation. Often the "right" to teach and engage in the practice of critique requires running some kind of time consuming vocationally orientated service course or consultancy based research project to justify the existence of a department. It would be a mistake to argue that the political will of a few people working against the tide somehow indicates a healthy system.

In South Africa, as in the rest of the continent, the most militant resistance to neoliberal policies in higher education has been directed towards the exclusion of poor students from universities. Many of the struggles against apartheid developed around education or placed demands for free access to quality relevant education at the center of their demands. During the late 1980s and early 1990s when the apartheid state was losing the capacity to govern, thousands of poor students were able to force their way into historically black universities. Concessions were won with regard to fees and the rules governing access and exclusions and issues like the sharing of residence rooms. In a number of instances victories were not simply economistic. There was also meaningful progress towards developing a pedagogy of the oppressed, within the university and in relation to communities outside the university, as part of a the broader project of, in Mamdani's terms, democratizing as well as deracializing institutions.[27] Annual revolts at registration time kept up the pressure on managements. This process continued into the early post-apartheid period but the political legitimacy of the ANC's "transformation" in the media and other elite spaces has steadily pushed students into a corner.

Widespread, organized and overt opposition to neoliberal policies has come to a head on a number of occasions. The most notable rebellions have been at the University of the Western Cape in October 1998[28]; at the University of the Witwatersrand early in 2001[29] and again in 2004; at the former University of the North in early 2004; and at the former University of Durban-Westville (UDW) in 1998 and again on the morning of May 16, 2000, when a student, Michael Makhabane, was shot dead by the police during a peaceful protest against the exclusion of poor students from the University. The murder was greeted with an orgy of elite condemnation of UDW students and, despite ongoing protests by staff and students, the police officer responsible for the shooting has still not been charged. This stark fact compels us to reject the idea that the threats to academic freedom generated by commodification are only economic. This true in so far as organizations and books and political tendencies are no longer banned in South Africa. However there is a point at which economics has to articulate itself politically and materially. A number of critical academics have been fired under scandalous circumstances in the last ten years[30] and a number of others have come close to a similar fate; a number of critical student tutors have not had contracts renewed; radical students have been expelled from universities and there has been serious and often violent repression of student resistance to the exclusion of poor student. University managements have undertaken a range of other repressive actions over the last ten years that include various forms of intimidation, monitoring staff emails and so on.

Most of the gains with regard to democratization won in the late 1980s and early 1990s have been undone as universities were rapidly corporatized in terms of their governance and commodified in terms of their work from the mid 1990s. Overt resistance does continue, in the face of wide condemnation by the media and university councils stacked with business and political elites, but has largely been reduced to technical and economic issues - fee structures, payment schedules and so on.[31] As I write the GaRankuwa campus of the newly merged Tshwane University of Technology is closed after students took staff hostage and burnt three lecture halls in protest at exclusions due to increasing fees.[32] A few weeks ago the students at the University of the Witwatersrand were in revolt. There have also been a series of militant and ongoing struggles against the exploitation and retrenchment of workers.[33] Many people wage covert struggles against commodification by allowing students to illegally photocopy readings, attend classes without paying fees and use African languages in class and in written work. There is also resistance, again often covert, against neo-colonial curricula with lecturers and tutors smuggling critical ideas into courses presented to the mandarins in instrumental terms. But overt contestation around democratization has largely been crushed.

South African students and workers have a brave record of resisting neoliberalism in post-apartheid universities. However with a few notable exceptions South African academics have failed to take up issues of academic freedom in the post-apartheid era with much vigor. Some of the academics who have done so have paid a heavy price and have lost their jobs. Many other academics have followed the consultancy route and become rich. These facts don't make critique, especially when it is linked to organizational action, a very attractive project. However we hope that this book, together with the excellent work in existing although fragile nodes of critique and academic/student and academic/worker solidarity, will encourage more critique from South African academics. The stakes are high.

Notes

1. For pictures of this march go to
   http://www.nu.ac.za/ccs/default.asp?3,43,10,1326
2. For an excellent account of the World Bank's devastating impact on African Universities See *A Thousand Flowers: Social Struggles Against Structural Adjustment in African Universities* edited by Silvia Federici, George Caffentzis, and Ousseina Alidou (Trenton, NJ: African World Press, 2000).
3. *Committee for Academic Freedom in Africa Newsletter* no. 17 Fall 2001/Winter 2002. pg 1.
4. *Ibid.*
5. For more on this see Adebayo Olukoshi and Paul Tiyambe Zeleza's introduction to their edited collection, *African Universities in the Twenty First Century* (Dakar : CODESRIA, 2004).
6. For a detailed argument in this regard see Richard Pithouse, "Producing the Poor: The World Bank's New Discourse of Domination," *African Sociological Review* Vol. 7. No. 2. (2003), pp. 118 - 148.
7. G. Arrighi, 'The African Crisis', *New Left Review* (2002), p. 15, www.newleftreview.net, p. 4.
8. See William Robinson, *Promoting Polyarchy: Globalization, US intervention and hegemony* for a persuasive and detailed account of this.
9. See *Harmonisation and Coherence: White Knights or Trojan Horses?* Bretton Woods Project.
10. Mahmood Mamdani, "Research and Transformation: Reflections on a Visit to South Africa." Seminar given at the Center for Basic Research, Kampala, February 1992 cited in Gregory Anderson, *Building a People's University in South Africa* (New York: Peter Lang, 2002), p. 50.

11. Adebayo Olukoshi and Paul Tiyambe Zeleza, *African Universities in the Twenty First Century* (Dakar: CODESRIA, 2004), p. 3.
12. For an interesting case study of Makere University see Quintas Oula Obong, "Academic dilemmas under neo-liberal education reforms: A review of Makerere University, Uganda," in Olukoshi and Zeleza, *African Universities in the Twenty first Century*.
13. This is detailed in Patrick Bond's *Elite Transition* (London: Pluto Press, 2000).
14. For an argument in this regard see Ashwin Desai and Richard Pithouse, "What Stank in the Past is the Present's Perfume," *South Atlantic Quarterly* (Fall 2004) Vol. 103, No.4, pp. 841-882.
15. Again, see Patrick Bond's work including his most recent book *Talk Left Walk Right* (Pietermaritzburg: University of KwaZulu-Natal Press, 2004).
16. See Nigel Gibson, *Fanon, Marx and the New Reality of the Nation: Black political empowerment and the challenges of a new humanism in South Africa.* (The Annual Frantz Fanon lecture: Durban, July 2004).
17. Jonathan Jansen, "Mergers in South African higher education: theorising change in transitional contexts," *Politikon* Vol. 30. No1. (2002), p. 38.
18. For a fuller argument in this regard see Richard Pithouse, "Asmal's Merger Plans: Critical Choices," *Quarterly Review of Education*(2002),Volume 9, No.2: 32-35.
19. See "Where is the Grand Plan?" *Mail & Guardian*, 27 August 2004, p. 28.
20. Fazel Khan, *Merger's Neoliberal Soul Emerges from the Mists of Transformation Rhetoric* unpublished, 2004.
21. Karl Marx *Capital: A Critique of Political Economy* Vol.3. (New York: Penguin, 1976), p. 736.
22. This argument about the World Bank's new discourse is developed in full in Richard Pithouse, "Producing the Poor: The World Bank's new discourse of domination," *Banking Against Hegemony* edited by David Moore, (forthcoming)
23. Fanon, *The Wretched of the Earth*, p. 31
24. "Shock UN ranking of SA below Palestine," *This Day* July 16, 2004, p. 3.
25. South African Association of Political Studies Biennial Congress 2004, *Call for papers.*
26. *This Day*, July 20, 2004, p. 7.

27. For an account of struggles and resistance at the Univeristy of the Western Cape see Gregory Anderson, *Building a People's University in South Africa.*

28. See Andrew Nash, "Neo-liberal Restructuring and the Struggle at the University of the Western Cape," *Committee for Academic Freedom Newsletter* No. 16., p 3 - 9.

29. For a good account of this and the process of university commodification in general see Franco Barchiesi "Lean and Very Mean - Restructuring Wits University" *Southern Africa Report* Vol. 15, No.4, pp. 24 – 26; and Franco Barchiesi, "The Lean and Mean University: Tertiary Education and the Rise of Managerialism," *Committee for Academic Freedom Newsletter* No. 16. p 10 - 19.

30. Most notably Robert Shell, Caroline White and Ashwin Desai.

31. Although the Socialist Student Movement, active at the University of the Witwatersrand and the Westville Campus of the University of KwaZulu-Natal, has an exemplary record of effectively and clearly linking student struggles to broader social struggles.

32. 'Tshwane campus shut after torching' *This Day*, July 23, 2004, p. 3.

33. For a history of some of these struggles see Bridget Kenny and Marlea Clarke, "University Workers - Exclude them Out," *Southern Africa Report* Vol. 14, No. 4 pp. 27 - 30 and for the background to these struggles see van der Walt, Lucien; Bolsmann, Chris; Johnson, Bernadette and Martin, Lindsey, "On The Outsourced University: A survey of the rise of support service outsourcing in public sector higher education in South Africa, and its effects on workers and trade unions, 1994 – 2001," *Sociology of Work Unit*, University of the Witwatersrand (2002): 1-46. http://www.ukzn.ac.za/ccs

Part One

From Autonomy to Managerialism

Restructuring South African Universities

Andrew Nash

The framework for restructuring of higher education in South Africa was announced on February 11, 2002, by a National Working Group that had been appointed by the Minister of Education and was chaired by Saki Macozoma, a former political prisoner and ANC member of parliament and now a prominent businessman. The framework was adopted, with some significant modifications, by a meeting of the South African cabinet on May 30, 2002. It represents the most important change in the higher education landscape in South Africa since the introduction of university apartheid in 1959, and will shape developments in South African universities for decades to come.

The main feature of this framework is the reduction of institutions for higher education from thirty-six to twenty-one, mainly through mergers of currently existing universities and technikons. By the time of the announcement, agricultural, nursing, and teaching training colleges had already been incorporated into neighboring universities. The framework also proposed a greater differentiation of degree-granting powers among universities, limiting the number of universities that can now award post-graduate degrees. After various attempts to find an appropriate terminology, all institutions affected by the restructuring are now known as universities, although there is a distinction between traditional universities—the main focus of this piece—and institutions that will be known as universities of technology.

The restructuring of higher education has been presented as a process of overcoming the legacy of apartheid—the peculiar

1

irrationality of racial division that was built into every area of South African life. There is some truth to this account of the restructuring, but it is far from being the whole story. This account obscures the project of class re-alignment that was an essential part of the transition from apartheid to democracy. The transition included the demobilization of a liberation movement with radical aims and a mass base, at the same time as the ANC government committed itself to neoliberal economic policies and to building a new black elite strongly oriented towards global competitiveness. Although the rhetoric of non-racialism and democracy was used to explain and justify the restructuring of higher education, this class project had a more consistent role in deciding the form of the new higher education system.

This is not to suggest that South African higher education could have avoided some kind of restructuring. By the time apartheid came to an end, the system was in chaos and many of its institutions were not functioning in a way that anyone regarded as satisfactory, or even intelligible. The situation was then exacerbated by years of uncertainty and confusion after 1994 as universities constantly drafted new rules and curricula in response to any number of conflicting, changing, and often muddled guidelines issued by commissions, committees, and the national Department of Education.

For those caught up in the process, even those who opposed this restructuring plan, it was still a relief to have the uncertainty at an end. However, even within the limits of the capitalist class project of the new South Africa, it is not so clear that this restructuring will provide a coherent solution to the crisis had overtaken higher education by the end of apartheid.

II

Although educational institutions change in response to their political and economic context, they also have historical trajectories of their own. In particular, changes in intellectual life are often slower than changes in the political economy and draw on the resources of the past in a different way. University restructuring after apartheid needs to be seen in a longer historical perspective than that of the transition to democracy, if we are to understand the crisis of the apartheid universities in all its dimensions.

South Africa's universities form the oldest of the modern, secular university systems in Africa, and probably the most developed in terms of infrastructure, research capacity, breadth of curriculum, and international linkages and accreditation. Higher education began in South Africa in 1829 with the establishment of the South African College in Cape Town (now the University of Cape Town). In 1859, a Dutch Reformed Church theological seminary was established at Stellenbosch and in 1866 a university college. In 1873, a number of institutions, were brought together into the University of the Cape of Good Hope, an examining body that awarded degrees approved by the University of London. Among these institutions, those at Cape Town and Stellenbosch were most prominent. In the years soon after unification of the British colonies and the former Boer republics in 1910, three autonomous universities were established-Cape Town, Stellenbosch, and the University of South Africa, an examining and degree-granting body based in Pretoria, with affiliated colleges in all regions of the country. In time these affiliated colleges became autonomous universities, and the University of South Africa became a provider of distance-education, with the largest student enrollment in the country. New institutions, mainly established in after 1960, were quickly given autonomy, although in practice they were heavily dependent on their apartheid masters.

Until sometime in the 1940s, the predominantly or exclusively white South African universities did in many senses form a national system, with varying degrees of bilingualism at the different campuses, a single national student association, and basic elements of a largely patriarchal academic culture in common.

Until perhaps the end of the 1950s, the leading South African universities ranked in the international second-tier— comparable, say, to the leading Australian, Canadian, or Dutch universities—and there was considerable interchange of faculty with universities in Europe and North America. In a discipline like philosophy, R. F. Alfred Hoernlé could move from the a chair at the South African College to Harvard University in the United States and then back to the University of the Witwatersrand. Similarly, J. N. Findlay began his teaching career at Pretoria, and later taught at Rhodes and the University of Natal before establishing himself as one of the leading Hegel scholars of the English-speaking world.

In the decades since about 1960, however, this situation has changed dramatically. The global context of higher education has changed dramatically since then, and at the same time South Africa's place within that global context has become much more modest and uncertain. Elite schools in the disciplines linked directly to professions with global standards—medicine, above all, and perhaps now business management—are the main exceptions. The current restructuring of South African universities takes place against the background of this decades-long decline. Although its authors give no account of this decline, except as a by-product of apartheid, they clearly believe that restructuring will reverse it.

III

Although apartheid affected every aspect of university life in South Africa, it was not apartheid alone that was responsible for the decline of South African universities. Apartheid created an ongoing crisis of legitimacy for all South African universities. In a period, after decolonization, when barriers of race were being dismantled throughout the academic world, racial barriers were being reinforced and refined in South Africa. Increasingly, it also ensured the isolation of South African universities, especially once the academic boycott came to be enforced in the 1980s.

The extension of apartheid to the universities also prevented the formation of a coherent national university system. In its place, there were three deformed systems, or perhaps two systems and a third in constantly interrupted embryo. The English-language universities—Cape Town, Wits, Rhodes, and Natal—were always predominantly white, although non-racial in principle, and strongly orientated towards British academic life. The Afrikaans universities—at Stellenbosch, Pretoria, Potchefstroom, Bloemfontein, and later Johannesburg—had an exclusively white student body, as did the bilingual University of Port Elizabeth, established in the 1960s. Fort Hare, founded in 1916, was for decades the only institution in sub-Saharan Africa where black people could get a university education. After 1959, in pursuance of apartheid policies, other ethnically or racially exclusive universities were formed for black South Africans—the University of the Western Cape for coloureds, Durban-Westville for Indians, Zululand, Bophutatswana, the University of the North (with various branches), Transkei, and others—each catering for its own ethnic category of African students.

The racial segregation of higher education did not affect university education only. Racial and language divisions were also built into the whole structure of academic professionalization that emerged after about 1960. In most disciplines, there would be two rival national associations—an Afrikaans-language association of historians or sociologists, for example, usually restricted to whites only, and an English-language association with a non-racial membership. Academic journals were similarly divided, ensuring that they could never become forums for genuinely national debate or provide a barometer of the state of the discipline within the country as a whole, its relationship to developments internationally, etc.

This happened at the same time as the U.S. university system was establishing its global dominance. This process at the same time created a new and dominant American model of the university, far more closely attuned to the needs of capitalism than the British and German exemplars it displaced. The American model's distinctive features include a highly-differentiated hierarchy of institutions, academic specializations defined in such a way as to establish precise norms of achievement and research "output," concentration of massive resources behind the highest achieving individuals and institutions, an ethos of individual self-advancement and undisguised careerism, and a strong orientation to the marketplace. For any university system to become "globally competitive" today means emulating this model. Most often, this meant using state funds to reproduce a system that, in the United States, draws to a considerable extent on private funding.

In apartheid South Africa, universities came to internalize the norms of this model but could never live up to them. Their failure to live up to this model was built into the system itself. Institutions were differentiated primarily on the basis of race and language rather than academic prestige. Specializations could not be coherently defined nor achievement within them measured by a common standard. Resources had to be distributed in accordance with ethnic policies or fantasies. In that context, cronyism was often the easiest way to advance an individual career. The only academic marketplace with a valid currency was international, and individuals were better able to compete in it by turning their backs on South African issues or even by emigrating. In short, the older, more patriarchal model of the university was swept away at the very moment that apartheid restructured universities in such a way as to thwart the new professionalized model that took its place.

University apartheid had all but collapsed by the time apartheid ended in 1994. By the mid-1980s the historically white universities had already begun rapidly increasing their intake of black students and by 1994 several of them had a majority of black students. White males continued to dominate academic positions, but pressures for affirmative action often took on a parochial tone when they went along with a largely conservative view of the university's functioning.

The historically black universities were always crisis-prone, but were often sustained by extraordinary levels of solidarity in the struggle against apartheid. After 1994, they were increasingly starved of resources, plagued by mismanagement and corruption, and left without a coherent vision of their future. The restructuring happening now at South African universities will merge most of historically black institutions with stronger historically white institutions-that is, the institutions best placed to emulate the American model-leaving their component parts to swim in the sea of academic capitalism or sink in the populism that sustained them before, but is now no longer linked to any larger social movement.

IV

The restructuring of universities after apartheid is intended to make the American model of the university viable in South Africa. Unlike apartheid, the new system will not discriminate on the basis of race. Nor does it introduce any overt principle of class exclusion. Instead, it relied on "performance indicators" relating to graduation rates, research outputs, faculty qualifications, financial resources, and the like.

Crucially, however, all of these indicators consistently match the major cleavages of race and class, as these have been formed by centuries of racial domination in South Africa. Rather than redressing the educational inequalities inflicted by apartheid, it generally follows the rule—without acknowledging it in so many words—that "to those who have, more shall be given." In particular, it benefits the historically white universities (HWUs) far more than the historically black (HBUs).

In this, the original proposal of the Working Group chaired by Saki Macozoma was more consistent than the modified decision made by the government a few months later. The original proposal left none of the historically black universities intact, while the final, cabinet-approved plan allowed for two of them—University of the Western Cape and Fort Hare—to continue.

In the final plan for restructuring, three of the four English-language HWUs will retain their identity as before, while the fourth—the University of Natal, which already consisted of separate campuses at Durban and Pietermaritzburg—merges with the University of Durban-Westville, one of the better-resourced HBUs, located in a major city.

The Afrikaans-language HWUs receive less favorable treatment. Only one of the five Afrikaans HWUs—Stellenbosch—will continue as before without merging with a weaker partner. But the mergers required for others—Pretoria with the Mamelodi campus of Vista University, and Bloemfontein with rural QwaQwa—potentially allow the original, far larger campus to continue its operations much as before. Rand Afrikaans University probably faces the biggest adjustment. The initial plan provided for it to retain its identity as before. But once Western Cape and Fort Hare were exempted from the mergers initially proposed for them, the revised plan required RAU to merge with the Wits Technikon to form the University of Johannesburg.

The HBUs will be most affected by the restructuring. Two of the nine HBUs will continue as autonomous institutions. Most of the others will merge with more powerful partners and can expect to have a vulnerable and secondary role within the merged institution. On the basis of conventional performance indicators, they will compete in a race for resources that they are bound to lose. One of them—Zululand, which had been plagued for years by scandals involving fake degrees—will lose most of its degree-granting powers. The initial framework required that Transkei would cease to exist, apart from its medical faculty which would become part of Fort Hare.

This restructuring is the central element in the remaking of the South African universities, but not its only element. The restructuring is also reinforced by a managerial ideology, backed by the national Department of Education and becoming entrenched on many campuses, as new managerial elites are created with minimal accountability to or ties with their academic colleagues. A language policy that ensures the dominance of English over other South African languages is mainly rationalized by attacks on Afrikaans as the language of the former oppressor, but at the same time links learning to the global economy rather than community needs. Systems of ratings for individual academics, primarily on the basis of research output, have been established by the National Research Foundation and are likely to influence every aspect of academic life. All of these developments point in the same direction.

For black working-class students—that is, for students from the communities in which the vast majority of South Africans live—it will almost certainly become harder than before to gain access to higher education. The bulk of those who get access to higher education will study at institutions designed to equip them as skilled technicians rather than independent thinkers—in effect, to provide the skilled labor required for capitalist profit rather than to evaluate critically the ends to which their labor is devoted.

What is certain is that those students from a working-class background who do gain access to higher education will find themselves in an environment where the needs and values of their communities are alien. They will find themselves in an environment that will require them to identify, in a thousand ways each day, with those who are wealthy and successful and disown those whom the elite excludes or fears. Their own communities will become objects of knowledge, but there will be no place for the idea of a university that empowers working-class people or provides them with the skills and resources that enables them to challenge their subjugation themselves. In higher education as in other contexts in the new South Africa, a decades-long struggle to overthrow apartheid and assert the ideas and aspirations of the majority has produced an outcome that will disregard and marginalize them instead.

V

We should not make the mistake of assuming that the restructured university system in South Africa will be more coherent than the apartheid system that it has displaced. Any system that does away with the overt racial division of apartheid will be an improvement. But that is not to say that the new post-apartheid restructuring will be a success, even in its own terms.

The success of this model of the university depends primarily on its being able to offer upward mobility to a growing number of working-class people in South Africa. It has staked everything on the university providing for the needs of the capitalist economy and rewarding those who do so. But both the economic policies of the ANC government and the restructuring program itself are aimed primarily at the creation of a relatively small black elite, linked mainly to multinational corporations, rather than a broader redistribution of wealth or opportunities.

The capitalist model of the university was established in the United States in the decades after 1945 in a period of widespread and growing prosperity. South Africa, even ten years after the end of apartheid, is one of the most unequal societies in the world, and its inequalities continue to run along racial lines. Recent research shows that white household income has risen by 15 percent on average since 1995 while black household income has fallen by 19 percent, despite the emergence in the same period of a group of black millionaires. It is hard to imagine that campuses will be orderly and productive when students find themselves accumulating debt to pay their fees with little prospect of a decent job after graduation.

An increased focus on measuring the research output of individual academics and institutions will also have contradictory effects. In a context in which publication in a small number of prestigious journals, based mainly in Britain and the United States, is the measure of success, academics whose research responds to the concrete problems of their own social context will effectively be penalized for doing so. In a context in which the academic marketplace is dominated by a handful of wealthy countries, the capitalist model of the university is at the same time a model for the colonization of academic life.

It will also be impossible to keep the contradictions of this ethos of self-advancement out of the curriculum. It will be easier for academics to publish work in international journals that, for example, interprets the work of a little-known poet or novelist in the light of whatever literary theory is currently fashionable than to publish work on the major works of world literature that is insightful but not path-breaking. Conscientious teaching and wide-ranging engagement with their subject-matter is unlikely to be rewarded. Unlike in a university system like that of the United States, with massive resources at its disposal and control over its major sources of publication, academic specialization in a smaller and poorer university system will tend to encourage work on marginal but publishable topics and give low priority to such tasks as teaching of the basic elements of the disciplines. It will be a policy of burning the furniture to keep the house warm.

As it happens, South Africa is turning to the American model of the university at the moment that this model is faltering, even unraveling, in its own homeland. Having fueled the growth of global inequality for decades, the United States is now re-importing the pattern, and growing inequality in the United States is making itself felt in U.S. higher education. Tuition fees are rising, subsidies are being cut, and all but the most prestigious U.S. universities are depending on an army of adjunct teachers, with low pay, no benefits, no security of tenure, and no stake in the life of their universities, often working for several employers at once. At the same time, the academy is under constant attack from a political establishment determined to limit federal funding for regional studies—above all, studies of the Middle East—to those that are directly subservient to U.S. policies and interests in the region. The achievements of the modern American university are extraordinary and in many ways unrivaled. But it is not clear that the model that has had such success can be sustained.

Finally, there is in South Africa a recent memory of a different kind of university life and above all a different place for critical thought in the communities that were at the forefront of the battle against apartheid in the 1970s and 80s. In those decades, oppressed people around the country saw that the official version of events could be questioned, that ideologies and institutions could be analyzed from their own perspectives, and that ideas and arguments could be a weapon in their collective struggle for liberation. At schools and universities these conceptions were developed and embodied in courses, seminars, publications, worker education projects, and the like. There was an alternative model of the university, however marginal and embattled it may have been. It is no longer a visible presence, and many would wish to forget it. But events could still awaken its memory and bring its energies back into play.

Accounting for Autonomy

Jonathan D. Jansen

I recently and informally polled a number of sitting and past Vice Chancellors as well as senior university administrators on the question: "Are South African universities less autonomous today than they were before 1994?" With one exception, all of them agreed that this was indeed the case; that universities enjoy less autonomy today than under apartheid. This immediately raises a series of follow-up questions. First, what exactly is the substance or content of this loss of autonomy? Second, how did this erosion of autonomy happen; in other words, what were the forces that enabled this loss of autonomy within the universities? And third, if autonomy was such a prized attribute in the institutional struggle against apartheid, why is there so little public outcry against the erosion of what T.B. Davie in his eloquent and durable formulation described as the right to decide who shall teach, what we teach, how we teach, and whom we teach? To respond to these questions it might be useful to begin by making explicit some starting claims and assumptions which I hold about the relationship between the state and universities.

What Happened?

The core of my argument today is that the most important changes in South African higher education since 1994 are not to be found in the dramatic structural reorganization of the sector or in the impressive policy/planning apparatus created for public institutions. Rather, I contend that the most far reaching changes in higher education are to be found in the gradual but systematic erosion of historical standards of autonomy that were ingrained within the institutional fabric of universities. Moreover, this erosion of autonomy within universities can be located within a steady series of specific events which, when taken together, have fundamentally altered the ways in which we talk about "the university" in contemporary South Africa.

I do not wish to underplay the significance of the merging of universities and technikons. Indeed, this is a major event in the post-1994 period that has promised to alter the landscape within which higher education operates. But our research suggests that in the long term, the most important effect of mergers may be, quite simply, the physical combination of two former entities (or the disappearance of at least one of them) rather than a recasting of institutional cultures or programs or profiles or productivities.[1] Whatever the noble goals espoused for mergers by officialdom, it turns out that even the physical combination of facilities may not be attainable on a grand scale because of the underestimation of the costs of these mergers.

Nor do I claim that the formidable policy and planning infrastructure set in place by the new government is irrelevant. We have profound and moving policy platforms and finely honed planning positions such as those evident in the *National Plan on Higher Education*. But there is considerable evidence that, apart from the blunt instrument of state financing, there is a very weak theory of action to translate the noble goals of policy or specific targets set in planning into institutional reality. In fact, it could be argued that the state is about to renege on one of the most sacred commitments of its policy—to dramatically increase participation in higher education—by prematurely setting caps on the number of students that may be admitted.

Quietly but steadily, the state has made significant incursions into the arena of institutional autonomy which fundamentally redefine the long-held understandings of institutional identity and autonomy. What are the specific actions which have contributed to this receding line of autonomy once bitterly defended within universities?

1. The state now decides *what* can be taught, or rather, what institutions might be willing to teach without subsidized income, through skilful manipulation of the funding formula. What the "program and qualifications mix" exercise does, in

effect, is to authorize the state to decide what can be taught where, if at all, irrespective of the local demand or institutional capacity. Moreover, an unprecedented flourish of bureaucratic structures—the South African Qualifications Authority, the Council on Higher Education, the Department of Education—now create a series of approval barriers that must be scaled in order to have any new program or qualification approved. So, it is not only that decisions about what can be taught are now centralized, but that structures of bureaucratic compliance ensure that institutions act in accordance with such authority.

2. The state now decides *which institutions will offer what programs.* For example, the decision to close Mining Engineering at the University of Pretoria and transfer that responsibility solely to Wits University is a case in point. It is not only that the state withholds funding from new proposed programs, but that it has taken it upon itself to close down existing ones.

3. The state now decides *who* can be taught, or rather, how many students are allowed to enter universities and in which specific fields. As already mentioned, the recent cap placed on student enrollments cannot be read other than as an official retreat in the face of declining central funds from a fundamental commitment of the White Paper on Higher Education—that is, the goal of increasing access to higher education. What is significant, for the purposes of this presentation, is the impact of the decision on *institutional autonomy* rather than the merits or otherwise of the policy itself.

4. The state now decides *how* students will be taught by placing institutional qualifications on a national framework grid through which qualifications are organized and delivered. The requirement that learning outcomes should be specified, that assessment criteria should be made explicit, and that programs should be "packaged" in particular ways are unprecedented intrusions into actions that were always considered the domain of the universities. Again, the issue for now is not whether such state interventions hold educational value or not; the point is that further ground has been lost in traditional areas of institutional autonomy.

5. The state decides on *which programs will be funded at what levels—but in ways that appear increasingly arbitrary* such as the differential funding decision on what kinds of programs are

more desirable than others e.g., the funding formula privileging masters degrees by dissertation only, over those in which theoretical training takes the form of coursework—irrespective of whether the latter course of action strengthens and deepens the quality of the thesis research being submitted.

6. The state decides on the *credibility* of qualifications, programs, and even institutions through the mechanism of higher education quality audits. What was until now the province of self-regulation among institutions is now the prerogative of the state. Despite the attempted reassurances that auditing is a mechanism for institutional development, the fact is that this form of state intervention could close down institutions or programs and make harsh and final public judgments about them.

7. The state now decides *which institutions will exist*, and in what combinations. The mergers generated fierce resistance from some quarters and this may also account for some reversals in the more ambitious plans of the former Minister. With the strong moral argument that the existing institutional arrangements reflected "the geopolitical landscape of apartheid", a politician decided on which institutions would be closed, which would be merged, and which would—in the language of the times—be left untouched.

8. The state now contemplates the *centralizing of information* (or rather de-institutionalizing information) required for student admissions in a proposed central applications office. There is considerable suspicion on the part of institutions that the real intent of the state was to push for a central *admissions* office—based largely on a distrust of institutions.

9. The state can now displace a Vice Chancellor on the basis of review and *install its own Administrator* to run the institution. An institution deemed to be in crisis, and unable to resolve such crisis, could be subjected to direct government intervention that changes key personnel—all allowed under revised higher education legislation.

I am not making the argument that some of these interventions were unnecessary or avoidable or intentionally pernicious; nor am I arguing that some of these interventions actually changed institutional practice. Institutions have become quite adept at dodging policies they do not like. For example, there is some evidence emerging that the national qualifications framework has had very little impact on universities despite its profound ambitions with respect to access and mobility of learners.

What I *am* arguing is, first, that these interventions by the state, taken together, have irrevocably changed the discourses, understandings, and behaviors of institutions in ways that make *any* state intervention more legitimate than before; and second, that such interventions have permanently altered how universities understand themselves, their missions and their degrees (sic) of freedom.

How Did it Happen?

There has always been, and continues to be, a tension *within* the post-apartheid state between centrist and democratic tendencies in relation to society in general and, in particular, in relation to the governance of the universities. How much control should be exercised over universities, and how much freedom should they be allowed? These questions, curiously, also preoccupied the first major commission on higher education, the Van Wyk de Vries Commission[2] of 1974, where strong debates raged (including an articulate dissenting opinion by G.R. Bozzoli) on the nature and extent of autonomy of universities.

Parenthetically, it would be very useful to do the unthinkable—compare the so-called Van Wyk de Vries Commission with the National Commission on Higher Education in 1996 to examine ideological continuities with respect to the question of autonomy.

Then, as now, the paradox of autonomy in South African society and institutions has been the subject of much discussion —a university sector (at least the white institutions) that at once enjoyed considerable autonomy in relation to the apartheid state but which at the same time was subjected to the most arbitrary restrictions from the same state. In other words, I am arguing that there is a coincidence of orientations between state-centered thinking of the Nationalist Party and the state-centered tendencies of many new government officials. In this context, there might very well be a degree of political continuity between the de Klerk proposals for greater control over higher education (late 1980s) and the Asmal plans for greater state intervention in this sector (late 1990s).

Unlike de Klerk, however, the new government could claim legitimacy for its intervention on the basis of an outright electoral victory. It could also, as guardian of the crusade against apartheid, mobilize strong moral arguments for bringing the higher education system under greater centralized control through appeals to politically loaded commitments like equity, access and redress.

What facilitated this unprecedented level of state intervention in higher education and the erosion of institutional autonomy was the crisis of governance, especially within the historically black universities at crucial points in the early transition (1994–99, the Bengu period). In ways not seen under apartheid, several institutions started to come apart at the seams during this period. Dysfunctional councils, corrupt managers, violent student protests, authoritarian leadership, financial crises, hostage taking, campus occupations by private militias— all of these posed direct questions of the new government.

Did this new government have the authority to intervene, stabilize and restore to order the turbulence in this visible higher education sector? In many ways, the credibility and legitimacy of the new black government was put to a very public test in the arena of higher education.

And it responded by changing legislation which placed unprecedented power in the hands of government over universities. At this moment of vulnerability, it pushed through under an impatient and aggressive new minister, a series of interventions (mentioned earlier) that would not have been possible with a strong, well-organized university system.

With characteristic balance and economy, Professor Njabulo Ndebele reflects on this period as one in which "a weakened sector became vulnerable to determined external intervention" and found itself "caught in a whirlwind of inevitable regulation and control."[3] He ponders that this regulatory environment could result in "a compliant higher education system... [which would] undercut the objectives of institutional autonomy as defined in the White Paper for Higher Education."[4]

In this context, centralist tendencies within government "won." But it is not simply the coincidence of centralist orientations or the vulnerability of dysfunctional institutions that brought universities into this heavily controlled status. It was also a set of earlier decisions made by the new government to subject itself completely to the terms and technologies of the global economy. The new state would prioritize science and technology, build human capital through investment in high skills development, build strategic linkages with the Bretton

Woods institutions, reorganize its macro-economic policy on terms that favored international investment and local stability, and define progress in terms of a global metric of development— exemplified in GEAR. What did this mean for higher education? Quite simply, the systems of evaluation and accountability, the measures of performance and progress, the terms of academic appointment and contracting, the sources of academic authority and institutional legitimation, and the terms of funding of universities—all of these have their origins outside of the country, and defined the ways in which the South African state and its institutions responded to what I have called elsewhere (extending Neave)[5] "a transnational form of the evaluative state."[6]

The loss of autonomy has to be explained, therefore, in relation to global, state and institutional developments in order to understand why it might be so difficult to regain lost ground in the near future.

What are the Consequences?

There is the disturbing recent story of the Irish girl who auctioned her virginity on the Internet in order to raise the funds to pay for her university tuition.

Reflecting on the history of state intervention in African universities, the political scientist Adam Habib makes the interesting point that once the state gets into the university, it has no idea how to get out. The loss of autonomy, like the loss of virginity is, as far as I know, not recoverable once given up. This loss of innocence is the major consequence for higher education. Institutions now have to pose the question as to how they will manage their relationship with a state that has centralized so much authority in itself that what is taught, how and to whom, are now legitimate areas for official intervention. It is not, however, simply a case of the state not knowing how to get out; the more disturbing question looking forward is: What is to prevent a virile state now or an undemocratic state in the future from pressing for even greater control over the day-to-day actions, decisions and destinies of individual institutions?[7] To avoid this happening, and to regain ground already lost in the autonomy stakes, higher education institutions will have to face up to some unpleasant facts.

The first is to concede that autonomy as a historical and political concept is a two-edged sword. On the one hand, the struggle *for* autonomy enabled the white English universities, and in particular UCT and Wits, to declare themselves "open" and reserve the right to admit "non-Europeans" (as black people were then called). On the other hand, it was also a powerful instrument in the hands of institutions to determine how many to admit, to what facilities, and into which programs. The same argument could be made for staffing appointments. In preparing for this lecture, I was stuck by the deep racism, offensive paternalism, and the sense of European mission (let alone epistemological naïvete) that accompanied moving arguments by the great English liberal men for greater autonomy with respect to decisions over admissions.[8] Is it possible, therefore, that the racial distribution of senior academic staff at the former white universities reflects, at least in part, the negative consequences of institutional autonomy?

The second is to recognize that the infringement of institutional autonomy will continue unless the higher education sector as a whole begins to speak with one voice. Here we find a dilemma: in its politically crude and racially inspired attempts to rescue some of the historically black universities, the state has in fact "redistributed" funding in favor of these largely rural and underdeveloped institutions.[9] In the same way that the "open universities" were compromised by the silences and benefits that accrued to the Afrikaans universities in the 1950s, the post-apartheid university sector as a whole might be undermined in its press for non-interference by the silence and self-interests of the historically black universities. Unless the leadership of the higher education sector finds a strategy to speak with one, binding voice on the question of autonomy *as a common interest*, it will continue to lose ground on the right to decide on core academic matters.

The third is to be conscious of the fact that the universities will remain vulnerable to state intrusion unless they find ways of strengthening their own systems of institutional governance. The weaker the councils or senior leadership of universities, the weaker the degree of financial management and self-regulation, the less aggressive the measures taken to enhance student and staff equity, and the less democratic the forums established for stakeholder participation, the more likely the state will use such weakness as a pretext for greater surveillance, intervention, and control.

When Does a University Cease to Exist?

It cannot be when a government decree declares some final date by which a university shuts down, or when a large institution engulfs and extinguishes the identity of a smaller one, or when new signage goes up declaring an imagined community. Nor can it be said that a university exists simply because it goes through the routines of graduation ceremonies or that it registers another "intake" of students or even that it teaches them.

But you may recognize another university in which the entire place has been transformed into a commercial center, the departments called "cost-centers" and the students called "clients;" in which every "management" meeting is consumed with balancing the budget in the light of impending subsidy cuts; in which the response to external intervention is one of compliance and consent; in which the accumulation of larger and larger *numbers* of accredited publications is pursued with relentless vigor; in which teaching is equated with technology; and the mechanics of research confused with the elegance of scholarship. Just about everyone in such a place is in the business of (ac)counting. Here, too, the university has long ceased to exist.

A university ceases to exist when the intellectual project no longer defines its identity, infuses its curriculum, energizes its scholars, and inspires its students. When the intellectual project defines a university's identity, then only are the conditions set under which academic freedom can be secured and institutional autonomy jealously defended.

Conclusion

On the morning of the March 2, 1948, a 52-year old medical scientist born in Prieska stepped up to the podium of Jameson Memorial Hall to declare to his audience what he called his "intellectual testament" as newly appointed Vice Chancellor and Principal of the University of Cape Town. Speaking in the long shadow of the Second World War, the new man at the helm observed and then warned as follows:

> Recent history has ... shown only too tragically how easily and *almost imperceptibly* Universities can be deprived of their freedom until they become mere instruments for the dissemination of dogma and propaganda under

authoritarian direction. That no such degradation has befallen the Universities of South Africa is to be counted among our blessings; but he who thinks that no such danger exists lives in a fools' paradise (my emphasis)[10]

These words of Thomas Benjamin Davie are as true today as they were in that year when another nationalist party came to power.[11]

Notes

This article is an edited excerpt from *The 41st TB Davie Memorial Lecture* delivered at the University of Cape Town on 26 August 2004.

1. See J. D. Jansen *et al*, *Mergers in Higher Education: Lessons Learned in Transitional Contexts* (Pretoria: University of South Africa Press, 2002).
2. This is the *Main Report of the Commission of Inquiry into Universities* (Pretoria: Government Printers, 1974).
3. Njabulo Ndebele, "Higher Education and Political Transition," *IZWI Voice of HE Leadership*, vol.2, (2nd Quarter 2004), p.1.
4. *Ibid.*, p.2.
5. Guy Neave (1988), "The Evaluative State Reconsidered," *European Journal of Education* 33:3 (1998), pp. 265–84.
6. J. D. Jansen, "Targeting Education: The Politics of Performance and the Prospects of 'Education for All.'" 7th Biennial Oxford Conference on Education, University of Oxford, England, 2003 (forthcoming in the *International Journal of Educational Development*, 2004).
7. I do not believe that the political economy of South Africa parallels that of the post-colonial Nigerian state; but it is worth taking account of Julius Omozuanubo Ibonvere's (1993) account of how once great African universities can slide into positions of servitude towards the state; in "The State and Academic Freedom in Africa: How African academics subvert academic freedom," *Journal of Third World Studies* X(2): 36-73.
8. It is such attitudes that enabled the liberal E.G. Malherbe, for example, to point out that "These people are in many cases still close to the primitive mode of life; so that, as experience

has shown, they may take to burning down buildings, just as they burn down each others' huts in tribal warfare"—even as he lectured on "The Autonomy of Our Universities and Apartheid" (undated).

9. This is not a debate I wish to return to in this presentation; I simply affirm a position I have taken in the past that this rescue act is self-defeating for the construction of a high-quality university system even though it might satisfy short-term political pressures for the ruling party; a better strategy is to build a few strong universities from among the established institutions, and to accelerate their deracialisation as quickly as possible.

10. Inaugural Address by Dr Thomas Benjamin Davie on the occasion of his installation as Principal and Vice-Chancellor of the University of Cape Town on 1st March 1948, p.3.

From Racial Liberalism to Corporate Authoritarianism

Roger Southall and Julian Cobbing

> Higher education teaching personnel are entitled to the maintaining of academic freedom, that is to say, the right, without constriction by prescribed doctrine, to freedom of teaching and discussion, freedom in carrying out research and disseminating and publishing the results thereof, *freedom to express freely their opinion about the institution or system in which they work,* freedom from institutional censorship and freedom to participate in professional or representative academic bodies.
> —United Nations Educational, Scientific and Cultural Organization, *Draft Recommendation Concerning the Status of Higher-Education Teaching Personnel* (Paris: UNESCO, 2000).

Paragraph 16 (1) d of the Bill of Rights enshrined in South Africa's constitution lists "academic freedom and freedom of scientific research" as amongst the fundamental rights South African citizens should be able to enjoy. However, a series of disturbing developments within some of the most distinguished citadels of South African academia are now putting that freedom to the test. Whereas previously, under apartheid, the principal threat to academic freedom was *external* to the "liberal university" in the form of government pressure upon individual institutions and individuals to conform to state ideology and rubrics, the new threat is primarily *internal*, with academics becoming increasingly subordinated to administrators, who in turn are becoming increasingly intolerant of robust internal dissent. We identify this as expressive of a shift away from "colonial liberalism" towards corporate authoritarianism. To counter this threat there is need to comprehend it, and to explore why, unless it is resisted, it could have grave implications for South African society.

Academic Freedom in South Africa: From Autonomy to Accountability?

In a recent article, André du Toit has argued that:

> the traditional liberal discourse on academic freedom can no longer suffice: it is misleading in that it directs attention to supposed external threats rather than to relevant developments closer home; it is outdated in so far as the concern with institutional autonomy does not take account of the changed circumstances brought about by the managerial revolution within the universities themselves; and it is incoherent when applied to current issues of internal accountability and academic authority within the university community.[1]

Du Toit elaborates his argument around a critique of John Higgins' account of the liberal ideal of academic freedom, which revolves around the academics' "freedom from external interference in (a) who shall teach, (b) what we teach, (c) how we teach, and (d) whom we teach."[2] Whilst Higgins maintains that this formula remains as valid today as it was under apartheid, du Toit demonstrates its enormous inadequacies. First, the stress on institutional autonomy which lies at the heart of the liberal ideal is unable to cope with the increasing demands and regulation imposed upon universities in the quest for "transformation" and by the massive changes that the managerial revolution that has taken place in university governance over the last few decades.

Second, whilst under apartheid the government attempted to dictate to universities what students they could teach, the present situation is that the formerly historical white universities (HWUs) have not required official prodding to open their halls of learning. In contrast, a rapid process of Africanization of HWUs' student bodies has taken place, largely by a process of African students voting with their feet. To be sure, this represents what David Cooper has termed a skewed revolution, in that African students are massively clustered in the arts, humanities and social sciences rather than in the sciences, technology and commerce.[3] But the universities are adopting all sorts of academic development programs and scholarships to encourage black students to go into strategic fields. In this context, constant invocation of this aspect of the liberal formula is "at best ... simply outdated and uninformed .... at worst [it indicates] an unacknowledged hidden and reactionary agenda ... holding out ... against the impact of post-apartheid social and political realities."[4]

Third, du Toit argues that the most incoherent aspect of the liberal formula is upon its continuing emphasis upon the claim that academic freedom requires that universities should have the right to decide what shall be taught and how it should be taught. He proposes in contrast that some form of public accountability is by no means incompatible with academic freedom. Students, to put it crudely, deserve their money's worth, as indicated by longstanding practices in universities whereby external examiners or professional bodies play important roles in setting curricula and monitoring standards. Nonetheless, major dilemmas are now being posed by increased pressures from government and business for institutions to supply students and research which will enhance the international competitiveness of the economy. In particular, the shift from discipline-based degrees to more vocationally oriented "programs," together with an outcomes-based approach to higher education, has led to official proposals for setting up a regulatory framework to ensure effective external accountability. However, du Toit argues that this

> poses a double threat to academic autonomy: in so far as it is introduced and mediated by the managerial revolution it brings about first the displacement of academic rule by a managerial executive *within* the university, and secondly a shift from structures of internal accountability and peer review to *externally* oriented procedures and criteria for quality assurance.[5]

In these circumstances, although the traditional liberal discourse around academic freedom does not address the dilemmas posed by contemporary changes in higher education, no clear alternative conceptualization has yet emerged to take its place. Du Toit concludes, "The key issue for the current practice of academic freedom is *how to define and strengthen internal accountability, bearing in mind the growing pressures for external accountability.*"[6]

Our present purpose is to extend du Toit's analysis by arguing that the managerial revolution which is taking place in our universities increasingly requires that the managers must themselves be made accountable to *academics as well as to society at large.* This is necessary because, increasingly, the embrace of the idea of the university as a corporation is leading to the adoption of modes of governance which are steadily eroding the effectiveness of the traditional structures of academic rule. This includes university management's increasing propensity to resort to executive powers to secure the dismissal of academics that are perceived as "awkward" and embarrassingly critical of university power holders.

Racial Liberalism and Academic Freedom

Du Toit may query the contemporary utility of the liberal formula of academic freedom. But there is no doubt that it constituted the major defense appropriated by those universities which were opposed to illiberal intrusions by the apartheid government. At Rhodes, for instance, the statement read out at the conclusion of the annual academic freedom lecture, declares (inter alia):

> It is our duty to uphold the principle that a university is a place where men and women, without regard to creed or color, are welcome to join in the acquisition and advancement of knowledge. That it is the duty of the university to guarantee the rights of participants in the opportunities and privileges made available by belonging to a university. That the ideals of academic and human freedom are intimately bound up with each other, and that free universities cannot exist in an unfree society.[7]

At one level, such a statement is unexceptional, for even under apartheid the National Party government itself and every university, of whatever stripe or color, claimed their commitment to the ideal of academic freedom. Yet, as is now common cause, apartheid policies represented the very antithesis of academic freedom. Most notably, the Extension of University Education Act of 1959, which sought to proscribe black students from attending established (white) universities, led to the establishment of separate higher educational institutions for Africans, coloreds, and Indians. These historically black universities (HBUs) were characterized by grossly inferior facilities and were often located in obscure locations where, it was thought, the political impact of their student bodies could be contained. Yet, more to our particular point, HBU managements prostrated themselves before government policy, endorsed official ideology, collaborated with the security forces in the pursuit of order, dismissed or squeezed out liberal academics, regularly expelled student dissidents, and carefully controlled curricula in humanities and social science disciplines which might be potentially "dangerous." The inevitable result was that the construction of an ethos of authoritarianism in which the liberal idea of academic freedom was effectively obliterated.

In many ways, the model for the HBUs had been provided by the Afrikaans-speaking universities, where the academic and managerial culture had been constructed around support for apartheid, and which often provided the National Party with its intellectual justifications of segregation. As noted by Pierre Hugo, a few querying voices began to be heard in the 1980s when it was clear that white minority rule could not last for ever, but before that, Afrikaner academics effectively functioned either as vocal supporters of official policy or silently acquiesced. "A multifaceted syndrome of 'tribal instincts,' conformist conditioning, societal reward, ideological conviction and a natural human tendency to avoid controversy help to account for this outcome."[8]

The outcome of the racial and ethnic fragmentation of the higher education system was that it left the four English-speaking universities (Cape Town, Natal, Rhodes, and Witwatersrand) as the repositories of the liberal idea of academic freedom. This was scarcely surprising, for although in practice they played no less a role in the reproduction of South Africa's ruling class than their Afrikaans-speaking counterparts, they also deemed themselves to be heirs to the traditions of British academic life, and many of their own staff were either British themselves, or had pursued higher degrees at British universities, where they had absorbed the liberal ideals of university autonomy and self-governance. These, in turn, provided a platform for a repudiation of apartheid which, we would suggest, was as much an "English minority" rejection of the domination of political life by Afrikanerdom as it was of the subjugation of subordinate black races to legalized racial discrimination. In this context, dedication to the idea of the "open university" (i.e., one which remained open to black students in so far as the law allowed or could be circumvented) served at least two purposes. First, it provided an extremely sharp focus upon the practical meaning of academic freedom. And second, it served as a vital connecting rod to the larger global world of academia in the face of attempts by anti-apartheid activists outside the country to impose a boycott upon South African universities. Indeed, as the years rolled by, the international accreditation to which these universities (or academics within them) aspired rested precisely upon a capacity to demonstrate how they were "fighting apartheid."[9]

Nonetheless, just as Hugo indicates that the majority of Afrikaner academics were fellow-travelers of apartheid, so (we suggest) would a detailed survey of the personnel who staffed the English-speaking universities reveal that, for the majority, their opposition to repression was largely symbolic. We recognize, of course, that this is a very broad generalization. For a start, it rides roughshod over a host of existential ambiguities which their life-situations posed to that small minority of white academics (English-speaking and Afrikaner) who chose not to emigrate and who have a genuine claim to have posed serious challenges to apartheid. We certainly do not decry the bravery of those who risked intimidation, detention, even death, or just personal isolation in their pursuit of liberal or even liberationist ideals, either inside or outside the class room. Nor do we overlook the fact that, especially in the humanities and social sciences from the early 1970s on, there were an increasingly large number of academics who made a very significant contribution to eroding the intellectual confidence of the apartheid (and liberal) establishment, and who in some cases, merged a highly critical teaching and research into some sort of praxis by working for or with a variety of progressive organizations (black trade unions, the End Conscription Campaign, etc.). Life clearly threw up a highly complicated set of questions to those whose deeply held religious or political commitments demanded that they challenge apartheid to which there was a *variety* of ethical and political answers. Yet, despite these important qualifications, the adherence of the English-speaking universities to academic freedom was mediated through a prism of what we term "racial liberalism."

This is scarcely a novel idea. South African liberalism in general was widely assailed by Black Consciousness adherents and Marxists alike from the late 1960s, and allegations that the HWUs are still alien territory to blacks are still commonplace some seven years after the transition to democracy. For instance, Professor William Makgoba writing while he was at the University of the Witwatersrand, is cited by Hugo as declaring that the "open universities" should have declared their sins before the Truth and Reconciliation Commission: "A detailed and honest historical analysis of most English-speaking institutions would not only confirm the rampant racism and sexism still prevalent, but would often show how some of these institutions were even more advanced than the apartheid regime itself in seeking discriminatory practices."[10]

Makgoba's cry of pain is, of course, expressive of the fairly widespread view amongst blacks that the English-speaking community has been hypocritical in criticizing apartheid whilst enjoying its benefits, and that it is therefore often better to deal with Afrikaners, who if nothing else, do not walk around with foreign passports in their pockets. Yet it is also, at bottom, a straightforward sociological observation that although the open universities may have committed themselves to liberal values, their liberalism was filtrated through structures which were racially based. To put it at its most simple, the open universities were overwhelmingly staffed, administratively and academically, by whites, the majority of whom had political views which were probably little different from those of the large body of white South Africans. Most would have considered themselves committed to academic freedom; only a small minority, before the early 1990s, would have been committed to majority rule. Theirs was a liberalism which was qualified by their socialization into, and location in, a situation of racial privilege. In short, theirs was a "racial liberalism."

The Managerial Revolution and the Shift to Corporate Authoritarianism

The democratic transition has forced upon the HWUs numerous dilemmas concerning their need to become "demographically representative," so that—despite an accompanying debate about the need to "maintain standards"—it has become common for preference in appointments to academic positions to be given to "persons from disadvantaged backgrounds" and for admissions procedures in the "liberal" universities to deliberately "advantage" black students. As noted above, this process of "transformation" has been eagerly embraced by the HWUs, whose political legitimacy is enhanced to the extent to which they are able to now able to provide for the educational requirements of the emergent black middle class, which in so far as it has the capacity is now fleeing from the poorly resourced HBUs.[11] However, if the "liberal" universities are now embarked (to a lesser or greater extent) upon the project of becoming "non-racial," their transformation is simultaneously characterized by their managerial revolution.

The governance system which defined the "liberal" universities was based upon the ideal of collegiality whereby academics governed their own affairs. According to the myth which accompanied this model, equality co-existed with hierarchy, in the sense that the currency of ideas was supposedly weighed in terms of their rationality rather than the rank of those who had spoken them. In practice, of course, this ideal was expressed through the instruments of Senate, faculties and departments which were themselves constructed around a very definite (and patriarchal) hierarchy, with Senate as the mouthpiece of the professoriate and departments ruled by permanent, professorial heads. Nonetheless, despite the hierarchy, faculty boards most nearly approximated the ideal, as these made provision for representation of all members of relevant departments and, where consensus did not prevail, for majority voting. Deans, who were elected, were therefore notionally dependent upon their electorate and were expected to represent the views of their faculties on Senate. The latter, in turn, was chaired by a Vice Chancellor or Principal who—although responsible to Council (the body which "governed" the universities' non-academic affairs and which in a legal sense was the employer)—was essentially a fellow academic rather than a professional administrator. Indeed, key to this model was the notion that administrators were more lowly beings than academics, whose needs and requirements they were there to serve.

Such "liberal governance," if we can call it that, was inevitably untidy, uneven, and highly imperfect. Indeed, such a relatively ramshackle system—in which departments and individual academics enjoyed a high level of administrative as well as intellectual autonomy—could only work upon a basis of mutual trust, shared values, and professional ethics. In this context, resort to disciplinary sanctions to compel staff to undertake a particular course of action was rare, and indicated that the system had broken down. Furthermore, because this model was characterized by the relative autonomy of its parts, and because it combined opposites of equality and hierarchy, it allowed for relatively high levels of debate and conflict, and tolerated relatively high levels of administrative inefficiency. It was therefore most suited to the rather small numbers of students who attended elite universities and presumed a relatively generous level of financial provision.

The material and moral conditions which underpinned this model of university governance in South Africa far outlasted those which existed in Western Europe and North America, where the "massification" of higher education gained pace from the 1960s and hastened the adoption of new managerial systems and techniques. Restriction of entry to defined race groups, and the stunting of opportunities for Africans through Bantu education, meant that numbers attending university remained relatively small, at least until the 1980s. This enabled the state to provide generous subsidies, academics were relatively well paid, and universities retained their self-confidence. Meanwhile, the domination of academia by whites ensured that, despite differences over apartheid, there was broad consensus about acceptable modes of expression and behavior. However, if the stirrings of the "managerial revolution" are to be found in the need of the universities to deal with an increasing number of students from the 1980s, it was only to develop at pace from the 1990s, when—in the "liberal universities" at least—there was need for a new creed to replace the "opposition to apartheid," which they had hitherto flaunted.

Du Toit cites Bundy as observing from wider global experience that "collegial self-management by academics, to whatever extent it ever existed, is an historic form and not a current option."[12] To the extent that larger (and increasingly heterogeneous) universities required an expanding corps of administrators to manage their affairs and to implement more sophisticated academic planning, financial, student residence, and personnel systems, this was also clearly so in South Africa from at least the mid-1980s. As du Toit goes on to observe, this has significant implications for the idea of university autonomy, especially in a context after 1994 when the new government has laid much greater emphasis upon the national coordination and equalization of universities, while simultaneously subjecting them to budget cutbacks and more rigorous financial discipline.

In particular, it indicates an erosion of the authority of academics in favor of senior university administrators, and suggests that the stress on the institutional autonomy of the university "must by now presumably refer not so much to the realm for decision making by academics, but must in the first instance apply to the practices and policies of the new class of professionalized university managers."[13] However, while du Toit clearly identifies the shift in *power* from academics to administrators, he fails to explore the *authoritarianism* that has accompanied it.

It is increasingly a commonplace that, with the rise of the managerial revolution, the modern university has become more like an industrial corporation. In the words of Rhodes' former Vice Principal, Dr. Michael Smout, universities may not be businesses, "but they need to become more business-like."[14] As portrayed by Bill Readings, this corporatization of the university is not a neutral process, for in practice it is the accompaniment of globalization: "the generalized imposition of the rule of the cash-nexus in place of the notion of national identity as determinant of all aspects of investment in social life."[15] The university is becoming a different kind of institution, one that is no longer "linked to the destiny of the nation-state by virtue of its role as producer, protector, and inculcator of an idea of national culture."[16] It is becoming an institution in which the administrator rather than the professor is the central figure, and whose principal task becomes phrased in terms of a generalized logic of accountability in which it must pursue "excellence" in all aspects of its functioning.

Yet the idea of excellence is itself like the cash-nexus in that it has no content, and is subject to a wholly arbitrary set of meanings. The attainment of "excellence" can become the goal as much of university parking authorities as it can of academic departments.[17] Nonetheless, "excellence" lends itself, in particular, to the associated set of ideas around "quality measurement" and can lead to rankings of universities according to wealth, library facilities, graduation rates, publications, and so on—which leads, ironically, to an emphasis upon *quantity* rather than *quality*, the very obverse of the logic which "excellence" seeks to pursue![18]

Even so, for all its vacuousness, "excellence" is something that can be "marketed" to "consumers"—whether these are students, governments, sponsors, or donors. University crests, symbols of the medievalism previously cultivated by academic self-government, become replaced by "logos."

If the corporatization of the South African university has borrowed heavily from Western (especially United Kingdom) universities' experience, it has also been closely associated with the neoliberal strategies adopted since 1996 onwards by the ANC-led government which have adopted as their particular goal, the adjustment of the South African economy to the global economy. This has seen prioritization of "utilitarian" subjects (Information Systems, Computer Sciences, Commerce, Accounting) over the humanities and natural sciences. Meanwhile, this has been accompanied by the effects of the technological revolution which has simultaneously propelled the reduction of heads of departments or "program coordinators" to "middle managers," shifted increasing low-level administrative responsibilities upon academic staff, and facilitated the implementation of more complex financial and reporting structures—all of which erode the semi-autonomy of academics, and render them increasingly subject to central university control.[19] What Readings refers to as the proletarianization of academics is, in the South African instance, amplified by the particular consequences of the adjustment to globalization and the slump of the rand. Not only have academic salaries failed to keep up with those in the civil service and public sector, but academics are also increasingly expected to supplement their salaries by selling themselves on the marketplace, which now becomes the arbitrator of utility.[20] Inevitably, this is resulting in the devaluing of the humanities and the values—such as democracy, fairness, and justice—which they have traditionally elevated. And most particularly, these developments favor authority over debate. In short, the South African university is becoming ever less a conversation amongst the academic community, ever more a terrain dominated by senior administrators for whom academics are increasingly "human resources" to be redeployed, rationalized and retrenched according to how the university is "meeting the challenge of the marketplace." [21]

The Disciplinary Smothering of Dissent

Earlier reference was made to the differential traditions amongst South African universities which rendered the four English-speaking universities—although they functioned to serve the educational needs of the white ruling bloc—the major repositories of the liberal ideal of academic freedom. Most certainly, whilst the creation of the racially separate universities for blacks under apartheid had unintended, dialectical, and radicalizing effects upon their student bodies,[22] it would seem that the post-1994 crises with which the HBUs have had to grapple—notably financial cutbacks, corruption, mismanagement, and widespread retrenchments—have tended to endorse rather than to challenge their heritage of authoritarianism, even if they are now controlled by senior administrators appointed by the new government. Meanwhile, Afrikaans-speaking universities appear to have embraced the new techniques of corporate organization and marketing with alacrity, without fundamentally changing their ethos.[23] It is therefore the English-speaking universities at which protest against corporate management has been most overt, and in which the two most serious attempts to smother dissent has taken place. The first occurred at the University of Natal in 2000, when a distinguished, if feisty, professor of anthropology, Caroline White, was dismissed after a dispute which had its origins in an academic restructuring exercise led to her being convicted under disciplinary charges arising out of a tortuous conflict with her dean. For the University of Natal, this was deemed a necessary action against an employee who had been insubordinate and willfully difficult. For White and many observers, it was an assault on her academic freedom.[24] The second instance took place at Rhodes, where in its dismissal of Dr. Robert Shell, the university administration similarly insisted that it had taken wholly justifiable action against a reckless and impossible employee.

Conclusion: Academic Freedom and Corporate Authoritarianism

South African universities are responding to the challenges of declining funding, globalization, and the need to adapt politically by adopting corporate models of management, which are increasingly eroding former collegial styles of governance. This transformation is not only reshaping and intensifying the work of academics at the "chalk face,"[25] but is requiring them and the institutions they work for to become more accountable to their students, *external* accreditation bodies, government and donors. As du Toit has indicated, this revolution has major implications for academic freedom. For, while the liberal formula can comprehend external threats, it is inadequate to deal with the dangers posed by the displacement of academic by managerial rule *within* the university. Our analysis has sought to extend du Toit's thesis, by arguing first, that the liberal formula of academic freedom was in fact most elaborately advanced through a prism of "racial liberalism," and second, that an administrative authoritarianism, which is inherent to the new managerialism, represents a major attack upon academic freedom in that it aspires to subject individual academics to centralized control, and interprets dissent and criticism as insubordination, while itself remaining largely unaccountable. Indeed, the particular importance of both the Shell and White cases is that *they represent precedents which university administrations will in future be able to employ to inhibit or even suppress academics' criticisms of their actions.*

Corporatization of the universities lays claim to norms and practices that are universal, yet it inevitably takes on the cultural characteristics of the countries in which it operates. Its application is also highly uneven, reflecting the nature of the institutions by which it is increasingly embraced. In the South African context, where the universities have historically been associated with separate communities, managerialism has been embraced at a differential pace by the different types of institutions, with—broadly speaking—the HBUs lagging somewhat behind.[26] By implication, too, its embrace has been less traumatic at the Afrikaans-dominated universities, where there was already an inbuilt culture of authoritarianism. It is, therefore, not surprising that the crisis of adjustment has been most acute at the so-called former "open" universities, where the myth and practice of collegial governance were previously at their strongest. It is no surprise, too, that whilst these institutions have formally embraced non-racialism, that the actual practice of managerialism should have been adapted by, and adapted to, the racial residues of the past.

Two major points remain. First, how should we now conceive of academic freedom? We are certainly uncomfortable with the notion's elitist overtones, the suggestion that academics should have more protection than other members of society. Yet at the same time, we are more than aware of the dangers of eroding an idea of academic freedom which seeks to protect critics of dictatorship from oppression, not least in Africa.[27] However, what we do argue is the importance of including, within any development of the idea of academic freedom which seeks to beyond the liberal formula, the demand that *just as academics are accountable to their managers, so should the managers be responsible to those they manage* in the way, certainly, that they are not at the moment. We note in this context, with approbation, UNESCO's draft recommendation concerning academic freedom (quoted at the beginning of this article) which specifically includes the proposition that academics should have "freedom to express freely their opinion about the institution or system in which they work." We would further argue that the defenders of this freedom will have to be on full alert to prevent the particular intrusion of managerialism which seeks to squeeze academic freedom through the use of labor law and not least, the erosion of academics' security via increased hiring of staff on short-term contracts and the effective abolition of tenure.

Our final comment is that the defense of academic freedom against corporate authoritarianism ultimately lies in academics' own hands. The formation of effective national unions or associations, matched by active chapters at individual institutions, is clearly one strategy which is vitally necessary, and where South African academia, so long historically divided, badly falls down. Similarly, there is need for academics to demand that managements put in place proper mediation procedures which may prevent conflicts escalating unnecessarily, and which would serve as forum for *dual accountability*, of academics to managers, and vice versa.

As both the White and Shell cases demonstrate, defendants have at their hands, in the form of the media and email, highly effective tools for mobilizing international opposition to unreasonable managerial impositions, and for raising the costs to any institution of embarking upon disciplinary actions designed to shut down dissent. As both these cases also demonstrate, international networking may not prevent dismissal, but it can lay the basis for dissident academics' moral victory over their institutions. Yet, as both Shell and White can testify, following the shattering of their careers, *moral victories* are scarcely enough. The task for academics therefore, and especially in South Africa today, is to strengthen their defenses against authoritarianism and to make their universities institutions which both foster *dissent* and challenge corporatization by linking academic freedom to public debate concerning alternative and desirable educational and societal futures.[28]

Notes

This is an edited version of an article first published in *Social Dynamics* 27:2 (Winter 2001).

1. André du Toit, "From Autonomy to Accountability: Academic Freedom under Threat in South Africa?" *Social Dynamics* 26: 1 (2000), p. 128.
2. John Higgins, "Academic Freedom in the New South Africa," *Boundary* 2, no. 27 (2000), pp. 97–119.
3. David Cooper, "The Skewed Revolution: The Selective 'Africanization' of the Student Profile of Historically White Universities and Technikons in South Africa in the 1990s," Unpublished paper, UCT Centre for African Studies, April 2000.
4. Du Toit, "From Autonomy to Accountability," p. 95.
5. *Ibid.*, pp. 115–16.
6. *Ibid.*, p. 189.
7. Rhodes University, *Rhodes University Internal Documents* (2001), p. 20.
8. P. Hugo, "The Politics of 'Untruth': Afrikaner Academics for Apartheid," *Politikon*, 25: 1 (1998), p. 51.
9. As is made clear by Bill Cobbett's appeal for a flexible approach towards the boycott of "progressive academics" by the anti-apartheid movement in the 1980s. See W. Cobbett, "A Flexible Approach: The Tactics of Academic Boycott," *Work in Progress* 45 (1986), pp. 37–41.
10. Hugo, "The Politics of Untruth," p. 32.
11. But note that the student bodies of HBUs remain almost wholly black, and their situation is being rendered worse, in many ways, by the HWUs "creaming off" the most talented and better educated black students.
12. Du Toit, "From Autonomy to Accountability," p. 90.
13. *Ibid.*, p. 89.
14. Dr. Michael Smout (Vice Principal) to Professor Mala Singh of the National Research Foundation, October 18, 1999.
15. Bill Readings, *The University in Ruins* (Cambridge and London: Harvard University Press, 1996), p. 3.
16. *Ibid.*
17. Readings cites Cornell University Parking Services as having received an award for "excellence in car parking"! *Ibid.*, p. 24.

18. An obvious instance is that increasingly, funding formulae favor quantities of research output, in terms of books and articles written, over their quality.

19. E. Webster and S. Mosoetsa, "At the Chalk Face: Managerialism and the Changing Academic Workplace," paper to the Annual Congress of the South African Sociological Association, July 2001.

20. This also means the more rapid promotion of "useful" academic staff on grounds of their "market value" rather than their academic attainment, and the increasing willingness to award visiting professorships to businessmen. For a discussion of the implications, see R. Southall, "Americanizing Our Universities," *Daily Dispatch*, April 9, 1998.

21. Readings, *The University in Ruins*, p. 5

22. K. Adam, "Dialectic of Higher Education for the Colonized: The Case of Non-White Universities in South Africa," in *South Africa: Sociological Perspectives*, ed. H. Adam (London: Oxford University Press, 1971), pp. 197–213.

23. We are aware that these assertions about both the HBUs and Afrikaans-speaking universities are generalizations, which for our part, come from regular reading of the press and conversations with colleagues at these types of institutions. Our stereotypes are therefore very much a challenge to debate.

24. J. Guy, "Academic Quarrel Proves Campus Bosses Mean Business," *Mail & Guardian*, October 6-12, 2000.

25. Webster and Mosoetsa, "At the Chalk Face."

26. *Ibid.*

27. See, for example, K. Adar, "Human Rights and Academic Freedom in Kenya's Public Universities: The Case of the Universities Academic Staff Union," *Human Rights Quarterly*, 21 (1999), pp. 179–206.

28. L. Levidow, "Marketizing Higher Education: Neoliberal Strategies and Counter-Strategies," *Education and Social Justice*, 3: 2 (2001).

Language Policy, Symbolic Power, and the Democratic Responsibility of the Post-Apartheid University

Neville Alexander

Academic Freedom in the Era of Globalization

Important articles by John Higgins[1] and André du Toit[2] and Roger Southall and Julian Cobbing[3] have contextualized the discussion of this perennial question in both time and place. Du Toit, in particular, has put the cat among the pigeons by querying the relevance in the era of globalization and the corporatization of institutions of higher learning, of the classic liberal interpretation of the T. B. Davie formula deriving from the 1950s—i.e., the freedom of "the university" to decide whom to teach, what to teach, how to teach, and who should teach.

The gist of du Toit's argument is that the danger no longer comes from outside the walls of the university, in the guise of the racist apartheid state, for instance. Instead, the threat comes from inside the institutions themselves as the result of the so-called managerial revolution, which is a manifestation of the shift of power from the *collegium academicum* to the administrative officials, since the curricular and pedagogical—i.e., academic— freedom of the lecturing and research staff is thereby put at risk. He maintains that the manner in which Higgins and others have addressed the question is anachronistic in that the political terrain and the institutional dynamics in which universities operate in post-apartheid South Africa are light years removed from the apartheid university. At the very least, one-quarter of the composite formula, that which refers to "whom to teach" has been rendered irrelevant, since there is no longer any barrier to access to tertiary education, besides those that operate in any "normal" capitalist democracy.

Du Toit takes a calculatedly cautious view of the disguised enemy of academic freedom, the Trojan horse that has been introduced into the vice-chancellories and registries of the universities and somewhat earlier already into those of the technikons. His position is a cold-bloodedly realistic one. Universities, he argues, like most other parastatal institutions anywhere in the world today, cannot escape the logic of globalization, which is driven by the needs and the interests of transnational corporations, the latest model of the engine that drives capital accumulation. Whether we like it or not, principals and registrars of universities will have to become more accountable to those who provide the funding for programs and projects. These sources are increasingly corporate in nature, since transnational capital has displaced the nation state as the *raison d' être* of the university and of most other significant social and economic institutions. In the words of Masao Miyoshi

> (Whatever) remained in support of the coherence of the nation-state during the Cold War lost its rationale and efficacy at its demise in 1989. Global corporate operations now subordinate state functions, and in the name of competition, productivity, and freedom, public space is being markedly reduced. And the university that was at times capable of independent criticism of corporate and state policies is increasingly less concerned with maintaining such a neutral position. The function of the university is being transformed from state apologetics to industrial management - not a fundamental or abrupt change perhaps, but still an unmistakably radical reduction of its public and critical role.[4]

This is the spirit in which du Toit approaches the subject. It is, indeed, the spirit in which most academic staff at universities approach the matter. They have come to swallow the bitter pill of realization that we live in the era of "the market university ... where knowledge generated in higher education is increasingly used (and valued) for commercial purposes."[5] However, du Toit has the courage to pose some of the questions that challenge the complacency of the academy. In particular, he exposes the fact that the era is gone during which university academics were permitted to cut themselves off from the real world, which their endeavors were supposed to serve in the final analysis, whether they were aware of it or not.

To put the matter differently, if somewhat starkly: the corporatization of the university has foregrounded the fact that the university has a social responsibility, i.e., it is accountable not only to the collegium but also to various constituencies beyond its walls. The moat that secured the university from outside interference has been filled up by capitalist development and the inmates have to soil their feet by venturing outside beyond their comfort zones in order to address issues of immediate and ongoing concern to the people out there. I doubt that there are many who would not agree that this is most welcome. However, the answer to the question of who the constituencies are and what power they have to influence what goes on inside the walls is crucial. This mostly inarticulate question is the reason for the turmoil and the *angst* that has gripped university establishments all over the world. In our own country, the matter is contrapuntally underscored by the contingency of affirmative action strategies in favor of black, female, and disabled staff, necessitated by the peculiar transition to a bourgeois democratic dispensation from the illusory certainties of the apartheid state.

Not surprisingly, those who have discussed the issue recently have been most concerned about the "clash of cultures" inherent in the confrontation between the previous dispensation driven by collegial self-management and the emerging situation in which administrators and fundraisers call the shots. To quote Miyoshi again: "Higher education is now up to the administrators. And sooner or later, research, too, will be up to the administrators. Of course, we know that the administrators are merely in the service of the managers of society and the economy, who exercise their supreme authority vested in the transnational corporate world."[6]

However crude this opinion might appear, it resonates in the more measured tones of André du Toit when he concludes, "The key issue for the current practice of academic freedom is *how to define and strengthen internal accountability, bearing in mind the growing pressures for forms of external accountability.*"[7]

Changing the Software

In the South African context, the focus on the issue of who shall be taught and the related question about who should do the teaching, is understandable, even if it does point to a rather parochial horizon. The urgent questions that have been raised by recent developments in state policy towards universities—such as the death sentences passed on most Historically Black Universities by the merger process and the inevitability of student exclusions and staff retrenchments as the merger process advances—are what we might call the hardware of the system. As such, they are obviously of extreme importance. However, there are questions concerning the systemic software which, because they tend to be avoided, will come back to haunt us in the not so distant future, unless we begin to address them directly and without regard to where they lead us.

It is on this neglected area that I want to focus in this short essay. I want to use this opportunity to put the spotlight on the *how to teach* element of the four questions which constitute the T. B. Davie formula. It is the one question which is never interrogated, yet it is in some ways perhaps the most important of the four. I am not in this context concerned with logistical and delivery issues in the narrower sense. The point I want to focus on goes to the very heart of all learning: the language of tuition. The extent to which South African intellectuals have chosen to close their eyes to the significance of this question is truly incomprehensible, given the fact that anyone who is endowed with even a modicum of pedagogical imagination knows that there is an indisputable causal link between the mediocrity of South African intellectual performance, generally speaking, and the language, or languages, of tuition in our educational institutions.

For those who are determined not to understand the potential social dangers inherent in this question, it might not suffice to point to the fact that the language of teaching was the proximate cause of the Soweto uprising which, as we now know, heralded the end of apartheid as a political system.

Why am I raising this issue in the context of academic freedom? The answer is astoundingly simple. If I am unable to express myself fluently in the only legitimate language on any campus in this country, my freedom of speech and a fortiori my academic freedom are literally curtailed. Simple as it is, the answer raises extremely complex questions, which involve a radical reorientation of the educational system of this country. If we take as our point of departure the proposition that the academic requirements and practices of universities, because of the social prestige of these institutions, have a decisive backwash effect on all pre-university education, we will understand that the ramifications of any change in the approach to the language of tuition at the universities are necessarily systemic in nature. To put the matter beyond all doubt: *The core issue is that we have to begin to work out the implications at every level of the educational system of the need in this country to rehabilitate mother-tongue, i.e., first-language medium education in the school system. To put the issue in even bolder relief: We have to consider the implications of changing the language-medium basis of the educational system from a second or, for most South Africans, a foreign language to a first language or a mother tongue.* The fact that ten years into the new democratic, post-apartheid period we have not done so is an indictment in the first instance on the foresight and the sense of social responsibility of the tertiary educational sector. South African educators have to realize that the time has come to lay to rest the ghost of Dr. Verwoerd and to lead South African education back into the mainstream of global education. One of the preconditions for doing this is to rehabilitate what, for the sake of convenience, we can loosely call mother-tongue education as not only a valid pedagogical principle but even as indispensable to teaching and learning, an educational approach which is universally accepted as being the most effective.

The misguided rejection of this principle and this approach to education by what used to be thought of as a very large number of South African parents and teachers is the single most disastrous legacy of apartheid and colonialism with which we have to grapple in post-apartheid South Africa.[8] That it is a political hot potato is more than obvious. But, equally obviously, unless we tackle the issue aggressively, we are dooming countless generations of South Africans, especially black South African youth, to a destiny of mediocrity and failure. For we cannot repeat often enough the paradoxical fact that the only children in South Africa who are the beneficiaries of mother-tongue education from the cradle to the university are first-language speakers of English and many first-language speakers of Afrikaans. And every single year the results show up in the matriculation examination results as well as in the disastrous dropout rates which render most of our learners functionally illiterate. If nothing else, the economic costs of the system manifest in the billions of rands wasted annually in paying teachers to produce a 50 percent failure rate (using criteria which are pathetically low by any standard) should give us pause to reconsider the issue. Add to this, the social costs in escalating alienation, crime, and violence, and we know that we have to prioritize this issue and the related educational and socio-economic issues as a matter of dire necessity. In order for us to assess this adequately, it is necessary that we undertake a brief digression into the field of the sociology of language.

Symbolic Power and the Linguistic Market

The late French sociologist, Pierre Bourdieu, spent three decades clearing away the cobwebs that encumber our understanding of the relationship between language policy, language use, and political, economic, and social power. In order for us to appreciate the essential point that language policy and language practices in institutions such as universities inevitably either reinforce or counter societal tendencies towards the unequal distribution of resources, opportunities and life chances, it is appropriate that I summarize some of the relevant insights from the work of Bourdieu and his school.

To begin with, Bourdieu's notion of "symbolic power" is similar to the Gramscian concept of hegemony.[9] The term refers not so much to a specific form of power but to an aspect of most forms of power.[10] It is an invisible power that suffuses all spheres of social life in such a manner that the very people who are subjected by it are actively complicit in their subjection. In the words of John Thompson, one of the scholars who have popularized Bourdieu's work in the English-speaking world: "Dominated individuals are not passive bodies to which symbolic power is applied, as it were, like a scalpel to a corpse. Rather, symbolic power requires, as a condition of its success, that those subjected to it believe in the legitimacy of power and the legitimacy of those who wield it."[11]

The second decisive concept is that of "the linguistic market." As in the case of economic markets and to a large extent conterminously with their evolution, linguistic markets come about as the result of historically determined interaction between peoples who speak different dialects or languages. In the course of struggles, marked by the peculiarities of each individual social formation, one or other dialect, variety, or language becomes dominant in such a manner that its native speakers are thereby advantaged over others. This hierarchy of languages or speech varieties apportions differential value to each of the varieties concerned. Those who acquire competence in what comes to be viewed as the "legitimate language"[12] are said to possess a larger measure of "linguistic capital" than those who lack such competence.

> In a given linguistic market some products are valued more highly than others; and part of the practical competence of speakers is to know how, and to be able, to produce expressions which are highly valued on the markets concerned.... Different speakers possess different quantities of "linguistic capital"—that is, the capacity to produce expressions *à propos*, for a particular market.... The more linguistic capital that speakers possess, the more they are able to exploit the system of differences to their advantage and thereby secure a *profit of distinction*.[13]

Crucial to the understanding of how this market subjugates the speakers of language varieties other than the legitimate one(s) is the process by which speakers exercise self-censorship, a fact which arises from their completely rational assessment of what counts in the market concerned. It is this complicity in their own subjugation which is the greatest obstacle to any attempt to change the conditions ruling on any particular linguistic market. In order to do so—and any society involved in a process of radical social transformation *has to* do so—what Bourdieu calls the "linguistic habitus" has to change.[14] This is a similar process to that which Ngugi wa Thiong'o, writing in the post-colonial and neo-colonial context, famously dubbed "the decolonization of the mind."[15] Thompson's definition of the linguistic habitus is most illuminating for the purposes of this article:

> The linguistic habitus is a sub-set of the dispositions which comprise the habitus: it is that sub-set of dispositions acquired in the course of learning to speak in particular contexts (the family, the peer group, the school, etc.). These dispositions govern both the subsequent linguistic practices of an agent and the anticipation of the value that linguistic products will receive in other fields or markets—in the labor market, for example, or in the institutions of secondary or tertiary education.[16]

This might be considered by some to be a long-winded way of making the simple point which Ngugi made so eloquently many years ago in his celebrated and passionate essay on "The language of African literature", i.e., that the African intelligentsia "even at their most radical and pro-African position in their sentiments and articulation of problems... still took it as axiomatic that the renaissance of African cultures lay in the languages of Europe."[17] For that is indeed what we are speaking about here: the hegemony of the languages of Europe, in our case English, on the African continent. It is important, however, to realize that what we are experiencing as one of the most dastardly consequences of colonial conquest and the subjugation of the peoples of the so-called third world is merely a special case of a general phenomenon. That realization is the great value of the investigations of Bourdieu and his students, since it also points to the magnitude of the task that awaits those of us for whom the so-called African renaissance, the hoped-for revival of the creative energy of the people of the continent, is more than a rhetoric of convenience and of dubious diplomacy. In this task, the universities have a crucial role to play.

The Responsibility of the Universities

Bourdieu's problematic assists us in understanding the ways in which language practices and the language policies of states constitute vital connectors between the system of production and the system of social reproduction. It is completely logical, therefore, that the educational institutions—in Althusserian terminology, one of the main ideological state apparatuses— should be singled out as the decisive agencies in shaping the linguistic market in any modern capitalist state. It is unnecessary in the present context to belabor this point. Suffice it to say that every member of a university ought to make the effort to understand, besides the manner in which his or her own specialty is transmitted to the next generation, how the particular vocabulary and, a fortiori, the language in which that vocabulary is embedded installs, as it were, a particular software into the minds of the students. Given what we understand today of the relationship between the language(s) of tuition and the empowerment of the elite by means of university and other tertiary education, it is essential that, as far as possible, university teachers do a course in the sociology of language. This would have the effect of making every such professional aware of the enormous responsibility each of us carries simply because we teach in a particular language or register of a language, all of which we take as self-evident.

This is not a simple matter of effective pedagogy. It is much more than that, since it involves the very character of the system of reproduction, i.e., whether it is meant to replicate generation after generation the same inequities, or whether it is calculated to flatten these out. In the final analysis, the question is about the definition and the consolidation of a democratic society, i.e., one in which all citizens have not only equal rights on paper but the equal opportunity of exercising their rights. Put differently, I am suggesting that the university has to re-examine its essentially elitist character not in order to generate some populist illusion about a "people's university" but in order to use its resources and privileges for the empowerment of the urban and the rural poor. In another era, we would have said that what is called for is that the collegium should commit some kind of class suicide, not because this is the noble thing to do but because it is the only way in which the democratic responsibility of the university in a state engaged in a process of radical social transformation can be fulfilled. This implies, if I need to spell it out, a very different agenda from that which is being forced on the universities by the transnational corporations in most countries of the world.

Notes

This article is an edited excerpt from the D.C.S. Oosthvizen Memorial Lecture, delivered at Rhodes University on October 9, 2001.

1. John Higgins, "Academic Freedom and the Idea of a University," *English Academy Review* 15 (1999), pp. 7–23.
2. André Du Toit, "From Autonomy to Accountability: Academic Freedom under Threat in South Africa?" *Social Dynamics* 26:1 (2000), pp. 76–133.
3. Roger Southall and Julian Cobbing, "From Racial Liberalism to Corporate Authoritarianism," Chapter 3 of this volume.
4. Masao Miyoshi, "'Globalization,' Culture and the University," in *The Cultures of Globalization*, ed. by F. Jameson

and M. Miyoshi (Durham and London: Duke University Press.1998), p. 263.

5. Cooper, cited in du Toit, "From Autonomy to Accountability," p. 112.

6. Miyoshi, " 'Globalization,' Culture and the University," p. 267

7. Du Toit, "From Autonomy to Accountability," p. 129. Italics in the original.

8. The recent language survey undertaken by MarkData at the request of the Pan South African Language Board (PANSALB) has, however, put even this widely held belief in question. To quote from the official PANSALB summary of the survey: "The survey indicated that the majority of respondents (almost 90 percent) felt very strongly that the mother tongue should have a significant place in the education system.... Fewer than 10 percent of respondents argued for an English dominant education system." See PANSALB, *Guidelines for Language Planning and Policy Development*. PANSALB Occasional Papers No. 6. (Pretoria: Pan South African Language Board, 2001), p. 20.

9. P. Bourdieu, *Language and Symbolic Power*, (Cambridge: Polity Press, 1994).

10. It reminds me of a profound fact noted laconically by Halliday and Martin that "the history of humanity is not simply the history of socio-economic activity, it is also a history of semiotic activity." See M. Halliday and J. Martin, *Writing Science: Literacy and Discursive Power* (London and Washington D.C: The Falmer Press, 1993), p. 10.

11. John Thompson, "Editor's Introduction." In Bourdieu, *Language and Symbolic Power*, p. 23.

12. In order for one mode of expression among others (a particular language in the case of bilingualism, a particular use of language in the case of a society divided into classes) to impose itself as the only legitimate one, the linguistic market has to be unified and the different dialects (of class, region or ethnic group) have to be measured practically against the legitimate language or usage. See Bourdieu, *Language and Symbolic Power*, p. 45.

13. Thompson, "Editor's Introduction," p. 18. Italics in the original.

14. The habitus is a set of dispositions which incline agents to act and react in certain ways. The dispositions generate practices, perceptions and attitudes which are "regular" without being

consciously coordinated or governed by any "rule." See Thompson, "Editor's Introduction," p. 12.

15. Ngugi wa Thiong'o, *Decolonizing the Mind: The Politics of Language in African Literature* (London: James Currey,1994).

16. Thompson, "Editor's Introduction," p. 17.

17. Ngugi, *Decolonizing the Mind,* p. 5.

"Constituting the Class": Neoliberalism and the Student Movement in South Africa

Prishani Naidoo

Europe, May 1968; the anti-Vietnam war movement in the USA; Tiananmen Square, China, 1989; the anti-WTO protests in Seattle more recently—there are many instances in history that reveal the significant power that students as a force in society can wield in effecting radical change in institutions, groups, communities, and society more generally. This has perhaps to do with the unique and privileged position that students occupy in society— for a time suspended from the everyday regulation and acceptance of the world as it is, with the "academic freedom" to question and escape the ordinary, to experiment, even if in limited ways. While for the majority of students, higher education has traditionally been a safe space in which to advance one's individual position in a society, for a minority it has also been a space in which to fearlessly and radically question and subvert those traditions and foundations on which society is based. Although there are many instances where universities have been completely or largely subordinated to repressive regimes, it is also the case that, even in authoritarian societies, the idea and practice of "academic freedom" has created an enabling space or shield for a culture of critique and protest that has resulted in large mass expressions of and for change.

Historically then, student movements have emerged across societies to critically engage those dominant and powerful individuals and institutions in the higher education institution itself as well as in society. Depending on their strengths and

51

potential to do meaningful harm to those institutions and individuals, student movements have received different responses from those in power. But, over time, with the need for greater articulation between higher education and an ever-expanding capitalist ethic in society, "academic freedom" has come to allow different and varying degrees of critical engagement with the status quo, and the notion of "autonomy" has come to be mobilized in the interests of the neoliberal agenda.

In South Africa, in addition to mounting mass protests against the apartheid state and contributing more broadly to the liberation movement, students have come together in acts constitutive of serious shifts in strategy and thinking in the anti-apartheid struggles. The walkout of Black students from the predominantly White National Union of South African Students (NUSAS) in 1969, led by Steve Biko, gave birth to the Black Consciousness movement and tradition, and shaped a student movement in South Africa that was extremely critical and subversive of the apartheid and liberal white status quo.[1] The student movement also largely provided enabling spaces for critical debates around race, class, and gender and the articulation of these debates with the wider liberation movement. Furthermore, a discourse and practice of self-reliance and collective action amongst Black communities was to focus popular intellectual engagement in the 1970s and 80s around the questions of a radical alternative to apartheid. The student movement became a space in and through which an alternative society to apartheid was imagined and produced. In this movement, students saw themselves as members of collectives and communities, actively belonging to local civic organizations and the like, and the space of higher education was seen as a means to attaining this vision of a society in which there would be no inequality or discrimination. In this vision, higher education was viewed as a central aspect of a new society, contributing to the needs of all South Africans as determined by their collective will. Just as apartheid had produced a divided, differentiated and unequal higher education system best suited to its racial project, it was assumed that the liberation movement would transform higher education to meet the needs of a post-apartheid democracy.

The actions of the apartheid state (the banning of the South African Students' Organisation—SASO—in 1977, arrests and harassment of student activists, detentions without trial, etc.)

worked to unite students despite political differences and to unite students with other parts of the liberation movement, as armed struggle and mass action heightened against the apartheid state in the 1970s and 80s. But when the apartheid government released political prisoners and opened the doors for negotiation in the 1990s, divisions and differences related to this vision that existed from earlier times manifested themselves overtly within the student movement and the liberation movement more generally.

This article will explore the emergence and resolution of these divisions and differences in the student movement as they relate to questions of academic freedom and institutional autonomy in the context of the entry of neoliberal policies in South Africa.[1] In doing this it will show how the potentiality for radical critique and change present in the student movement (and in the positionality of the student) has been foreclosed by the dictates of "responsible governance" under a neoliberal world order. The vision of the alternative society imagined in the struggles against apartheid has been lost to the mantras of the market.

From Protest to "Constructive Engagement"

As the student movement has always located itself firmly within the broad liberation movement against apartheid, its political orientation has been determined largely by changes that have occurred within the liberation movement itself. While apartheid produced a radical, militant student movement poised for action against the state, with the unbanning of political parties and the release of political prisoners, debates and differences began to surface, related to the ways in which struggle and change should occur. The merger of the South African National Students Congress (SANSCO) and NUSAS in 1991 creating the South African Students Congress (SASCO) already consolidated the new commitment of student activists to the ideal of non-racialism espoused by the ANC alliance, and rooted SASCO within the Congress tradition, a tradition that was to determine the character of the interventions that SASCO would make in the transformation of higher education.

Some of the earliest debates in SASCO in the early 1990s surfaced over the path that the ANC alliance was embarking on towards negotiating a transition to democracy in South Africa.

Significant sections argued for a severing of ties with the alliance, as negotiations were not seen as a viable option for revolutionary change. However, such debates were short-lived, with the student movement giving its full support to the ANC alliance in their negotiations with the NP government. Still upholding its vision for higher education as contributing to the redress of the societal inequalities and imbalances entrenched by apartheid, and seeing the need for a completely overhauled higher education system, many SASCO activists were unhappy when the liberation movement agreed at the Convention for a Democratic South Africa (CODESA) to the protection of the academic freedom and institutional autonomy of institutions of higher learning in the new South African constitution. These activists argued that apartheid had deliberately produced a racially unequal system of higher education that necessitated change—processes driven and managed from outside (by the state), as those in positions of power could not be expected to change situations from which they benefited. In their minds, autonomy would allow institutions to continue unchanged and unchallenged. While for these activists the autonomy debate was lost at CODESA, SASCO would work hard to ensure that a process was put in place towards the development of a national framework for the transformation of institutions of higher education to hold institutions accountable to their responsibilities as public institutions. Little did it realize that the democratic state would in fact seek to transform and restructure higher education on neoliberal lines.

What the student movement failed to highlight in its critique of the state's protection of the autonomy of higher institutions was the fact that the state was able to use "autonomy" to transfer its powers and responsibilities in the sphere of higher education over to the private sector and neoliberal interests. Far from institutions of higher learning being autonomous, notions of autonomy under neoliberalism have allowed for the greater pervasiveness of the profit motive and the market in the sphere of higher education. The student movement, in choosing to focus on the need for state intervention in the transformation of higher education failed to use the opportunities provided by the debate to secure the real autonomy of higher education as a space beyond the market and the state for the independent production of knowledge. In fact, there has been very little discussion and debate within the student movement throughout its history on the possibilities for truly autonomous institutions of higher learning within a fully transformed South African society.

While the introduction of the neoliberal macro-economic framework of the ANC government (the Growth, Employment, and Redistribution program or GEAR) in 1996 was met with initial resistance from the student movement, critiques of GEAR and the ANC alliance came to be silenced and contained within SASCO, with the urge to contribute "responsibly" to the process of "consolidating the democratic breakthrough" quickly gaining voice.[2] In the early years of the ANC's ascendance to democratic rule, SASCO contributed not only to the massive recruitment drives for the ANC around elections, but also to the Masakhane Campaign, urging township residents to pay for their rates and services—a program designed to reverse the culture of nonpayment inculcated in the rates boycotts of the 1980s. In this way, the student movement, organized under the banner of the ANC alliance, came to take up the role of governing responsibly, adopting a stance towards the alliance which it characterized as "complementary and contradictory," allowing it to be critical of the alliance but remaining complementary to its overall goals and political orientation.[3]

> People's power will become a living reality where non-state mass structures are able to articulate the needs and aspirations of ordinary people and where the state is receptive to providing resources to ensure that they are met —people's power from below and above. This is not the type of resistance-oriented people's power that we knew in the 1980s, but the people's power of socio-economic upliftment. Conscious cadres of civil society (i.e., the organizers of SASCO and other formations) need to find forms of mass involvement that will ensure that the state will co-operate, but forms of action that are not disruptive to the extent that they weaken the state by causing instability and empowering counter-revolutionary forces.[4]

This approach would in large part contribute to SASCO tying itself to a policy process for the transformation of higher education that would be constrained by a predetermined and non-negotiable macro-economic framework in the form of GEAR. As the Council on Higher Education's Shape and Size of Higher Education Task Team write:

> Higher education must help erode the inherited socially structural inequities and provide opportunities for social

advancement through equity of access and opportunity. It must produce, through research, teaching, and learning and community service programs, the knowledge and personpower for national reconstruction and economic and social development to enable South Africa to engage proactively with and participate in a highly competitive global economy. The role of higher education in the defense and advancement of democracy is closely related to promoting good citizenship, a function that is accorded to it in the White Paper of 1997. Such a role is also intrinsically related to higher education's ability to deliver programmes that are essential to the promotion of a critical citizenry, and to ensure that the higher education system is firmly rooted within South African society and its particular development challenges.[5]

From 1996, with the inception of the National Commission on Higher Education (NCHE), the student movement engaged in policy consultations towards the development of national policy for the transformation of higher education in the form of the White Paper on Higher Education (1997) and the Higher Education Act (1997). At an institutional level, transformation forums involved student representatives in the business of transforming institutions according to the national policy framework. This led to a certain form of bureaucratization and a decline in mass participation in the student movement, and the adoption of less radical forms of protest action. Significantly, this commitment to contributing to responsible governance has seen the student movement actively suppress and contain radical actions from its own members and unorganized students or non-traditional groupings. It is the latter who have provided the most militant, although often unsustained, resistances to neoliberalism.

The "contradict but complement" approach, together with the fact that the possibilities for transformation of higher education have already been determined by an unchangeable neoliberal macro-economic framework, have resulted in the continued waging of predictable student struggles within the acceptable channels of constructive engagement (e.g., around financial exclusions) with the struggles of students taking on a routine and rhythm that is acceptable and tolerated by the powers that be, and often considered in the decision making of institutions through the institutional processes that have been established to incorporate student representatives into structures of governance. For the student movement, this has meant the complete submission of its approach to transformation to the neoliberal agenda—e.g., seeking solutions to the problem of student funding from the private sector—and the structuring of struggle according to the policy program of the ANC alliance.

In the "Size and Shape" document quoted above, the phrase "constituting the class" is used to refer to the changes that institutions should work towards in terms of the composition of the student body in order to reflect real commitment to redress. A quick perusal of any of the policy documents framing higher education (the NCHE, the White Paper, the Higher Education Act) shows how the neoliberal imperatives of higher education recognize the radical potentialities of students and student movements and work to constitute this class in society in such a way that these potentialities are contained or deployed in the interests of neoliberal rationalities. While "constituting the class" might represent the policy imperatives for redress as determined and imposed by "the democratic state" on institutions of higher learning, it also speaks to the disciplining and regulatory pedagogies that neoliberalism requires and the suppression of critique and knowledge production that might challenge the neoliberal order. Through the student movement's investment in such constitutive processes, its vision of a different society has started to erode, being spoken only in the rhetoric of tired leaders, no longer imagined or dreamed by a mass.

From Society to Sector, Community to Individual, Public to Privatized, Collective to Self

In "constituting" its class, the neoliberal ethic has had to undo many of the foundational commitments of the student movement, in particular to collective notions of society and struggle.

Free Education: While early commitments of SASCO to the provision of free higher education were underpinned by notions of collective ownership of and benefits from higher education as a decommodified resource, with a democratic state facilitating the equal participation of all citizens in its governance, present day commitments to free education flounder in a context of neoliberal fiscal discipline and national priorities. Earlier commitments to free education spoke also for the need for community service, viewing it as part of completely changed curricula and aims of the higher education system. This contrasts markedly with the present day ad hoc integration of community service into degree programs as means to reduce state spending in certain areas through the substitution of real jobs with volunteer students, for example. Today, with its uncritical acceptance of the constraints and limitations imposed by neoliberalism, SASCO's continued calls for free education allow it to serve its role as this newly constituted class—making a radical call within a framework that does not allow for the attainment of this call, thereby giving the impression that critique and radical thought is allowed when in reality it is already foreclosed.

In the acceptance of the duty to govern responsibly within a neoliberal framework, the vision of higher education as a collective resource to be used in the shaping of a new society slowly shifted to that embodied in the following words:

> Higher education has private individual and public social benefits. The former relate to enhanced employment possibilities, better salaries and benefits, improved working conditions, improved health and quality of life and greater capacity to participate in policy and decision making. These private gains also generate public (social) gains such as higher employment rates, higher savings, increased contributions to national revenue and incomes, greater workforce flexibility, a decreased reliance on government financial support, and more active citizenship.[6]

This understanding of higher education as generating both private and public benefits has come to structure many of the policy agreements reached in the consultative processes to which SASCO contributed, resulting even in the continued commitment to free education coming to be structured by it. Far from the complete decommodification of higher education that early documents of SASCO committed it to, today's calls for free education assert the need for those who are able to pay for their studies to pay for this commodity and for the state to pay for those who are unable to afford their own costs of study in return for compulsory community service in areas of need identified by the state. Today SASCO even argues for community service to be a way in which higher education opens itself up to small business development and private-public partnerships at the level of "community development."[7] Under neoliberalism, "free education" coupled with compulsory community service becomes a means for the state to deploy students and graduates in the interests of the private sector and to the ends of the market.

The overwhelming reality, however, has been that education has not been free. As early as 1993, the student movement staged massive national protests and subsequently entered into a process of negotiations at a national level with the aims of securing a national student bursary fund. The outcome was the establishment of the Tertiary Education Fund of South Africa (TEFSA) in 1993 and the subsequent National Student Financial Aid Scheme (NSFAS) in 1996. In the short trajectory from TEFSA to NSFAS, the student movement gave up any real hope of attaining the goal of free education. Right from the start students were asked to give up the bursary component of the scheme. Today the scheme offers funds to needy students in the form mainly of repayable loans. Far from the vision of a collectively owned and driven higher education system accessible to all those desiring it, the establishment of the NSFAS and the submission of all struggles for student funding to its parameters have rather ensured the complete individualization of relations in this regard, with higher education becoming a precious commodity to which individuals aspire. The loan system, rather than engendering a commitment to collective well-being and development, locks individuals in an often eternal system of debt that only further encourages individual development and solutions.

And the NSFAS has not dealt with the problem of student funding. On the contrary, at most institutions financial exclusions continue to be a perennial crisis around which SASCO is forced into action. While up to the early 1990s, financial exclusions were fought on most campuses through highly organized mass campaigns that characterized exclusions as an attack on collective access to higher education (embodied in the slogan borrowed from the trade union movement by students, "An injury to one is an injury to all"), today most exclusion campaigns are small and driven by individual problems. Student representatives have come to be part of the structures and processes of institutions that seek to discipline students in all respects, including financial exclusions. In addition, the student movement has been forced to find solutions to these crises within the neoliberal framework, often tying students into individual arrangements that lock them in to individual debt to the capitalist system—sometimes potentially for the rest of their lives.

Negotiations: As SASCO has entered into structures of corporate governance within a neoliberal framework at a national and institutional level, it has given up many of its commitments to collective ideals submitting rather to the regime of possibilities for individual change. We have already seen this happen with regard to the issue of student funding, with access becoming an individualized question rather than a collective commitment.

It is also true with regard to approaches to questions of governance. While SASCO's call for the legislation of broad transformation forums (BTFs) at institutional level was not very well enunciated or explained, it did speak to notions of collective decision making amongst a community of those with interest in the institution that extended beyond the dominant notion of stakeholders of that institution. However, in the manner in which institutional transformation forums came to be constituted (often out of the need to manage crises), SASCO submitted its approach to the game of numbers, with all processes becoming defined by the need to increase the representation of disadvantaged groups in existing structures of governance, such as Senates and Councils. In this process, the agenda and functioning of such structures went largely unchallenged, with participation in these structures ultimately tying the student movement and other progressive sectors to the neoliberal agenda that came to dominate the transformation of higher education. In the words of a SASCO leader, "In the early years, post-94, we dealt much with issues of transformation—our focus was more on creating democratic structures of governance, without paying serious attention to content. A change of faces could have been what we thought were gains at the time, but as time went by we realized that issues are with content."[8] In its entry into the policy terrain, SASCO submitted itself to a process that narrowed the terrain of engagement to a sectoral level by separating higher education from other "sectors" and that transformed the relationships of struggle from collective engagements and commitments to individualized ones.

Curriculum: Despite paper commitments to academic freedom, under neoliberalism, freedom in learning, teaching and knowledge production have all been circumscribed by the neoliberal agenda. With cuts in state subsidies to institutions of higher learning, the duty to become financially sustainable has placed untold constraints on institutions and individuals within the system with regard to course content and structure as well as research programs. Increasingly, degree programs have come to be structured according to the perceived needs and dictates of the market, as private sector and state funding have come to determine the aims of learning, teaching, and knowledge production. In this process, the humanities have suffered huge losses, and the strict delineation of disciplines and streams of knowledge production have restricted the parameters for production in this space towards neoliberal ends.

The most recent transformations in higher education have related to the merging of institutions in the production of several new types of higher education institutions. Without going into the detail, it is significant to note that this complete reorganization of "the size and shape" of the higher education landscape has revolved around renewed priorities and goals for higher education as determined by the neoliberal macro-economic imperatives of the state, with the need for higher education to produce graduates more suitable to the needs of the market. In this way, much of higher education has been "vocationalized," with the need for the production of "marketable graduates" being the imperative.

In this way, academic freedom and the enjoyment of the space of higher learning as a truly autonomous space for free and independent intellectual pursuit has become reserved for a few—and in most cases these few are determined by their ability to pay for this space. It is in this sphere that the constraining of possibilities and potentialities for radical critique and the production of radical subjectivities is perhaps most stark and profound, yet least challenged by the student movement and the left more generally.

Student Activism: Representative governance does not feature much in the minds of most students. Voter turnouts in SRC elections have declined over the years, with groups of friends, the most popular people, the best D.J. on campus, and so on winning elections. This has also contributed to the low voter turnouts. Consciousness needs to be built amongst students that SRCs are important sites of contestation through the building of student political formations. In the past, students had to be politically conscious; they had no choice. Today, there is a lot of policy talk and students are not capacitated to participate. Also, there is no space given for activism—you have to perform academically, and individual students are easily singled out and targeted for academic nonperformance. There is a new political context for student organizing and leadership. There is also the question of the character of the student body—today we have an apolitical constituency and organization has to be transformed to meet these new needs.[9]

With SASCO's move into policy formulation, negotiations, corporate governance, and its acceptance of its duty to contribute (as part of the mass democratic movement led by the ANC, and as citizens of a responsible civil society) to the process of governing responsibly, its character as a mass formation shaped through struggle has changed. Membership has decreased considerably, and SASCO has found it difficult to sustain its vision of collective action for a different society as struggles increasingly became the mandated responsibility of individual negotiators or representatives who themselves developed into an elite layer of activists with certain benefits and privileges that others did not enjoy, such as access to policy processes (which included flights around the countries, nights in fancy hotels, stipends, etc.), meeting influential people, and so on. In this way, the student movement slowly developed into a space through which individuals could gain access to a different kind of life and power. Today, many of the student leaders of my time occupy influential positions in government or the private sector, constituting an extremely wealthy and influential class themselves, bolstering the neoliberal order. Today, the student movement, far from representing a means through which a global alternative to capitalism can be imagined, itself represents a means for individuals to ascend the class ladder and become part of the neoliberal dream.

In spite of the hegemonies represented in SASCO, there have been moments in which the radical potentialities of students have emerged within it to question these hegemonies. Unfortunately, they have too soon been contained or dissolved through the interventions of the ANC alliance and the disciplining tool of the National Democratic Revolution (NDR).[10]

Resisting Constitution

The current character of the student movement has not come about without resistances to its constitution as a class working in the interests of neoliberalism. "Operation Litter" in 1993 at Wits University, in which the campus was littered in a show of contempt for its policies; the successful takeover of the University of Durban-Westville (UDW) campus by a democratic forum of workers and students for two days in 1995; the food campaigns at the University of the North and the University of the Western Cape (UWC), in which students without money to afford catering services at the institution looted cafeterias—these are all instances of resistance to the mantra that there is no alternative to capitalism. They have directly instituted claims to the private and reconstituted them as collectively owned or determined. They were, however, quickly contained, silenced, or "dealt with" through the interventions of the ANC alliance. As members of the Mass Democratic Movement (MDM) led by the alliance, the student movement was often admonished by other alliance partners for being too radical or critical of government. The most common charge was of impatience, with SASCO being asked to discipline its members along the lines of the NDR. In time, any critical voices within the student movement came to be labeled as "ultra-left," "counter-revolutionary," and "undisciplined," and dissent silenced. In addition, threats and expulsions worked to remove any voices critical of the ANC alliance from SASCO. In time, critical members also left of their own will, unable to find the space for their views to gain voice within the traditional formations. Many joined or participated in the formation of new social movements emerging to fight other effects of the implementation of neoliberal policies, such as the commodification of basic services.

Some of the most recent student uprisings (e.g., at Wits University and the Tshwane University of Technology or TUT in 2004) have erupted outside of and independently from the organized traditional student movement, suggesting the growing irrelevance of SASCO in the lives of students who organize and act independently when the need arises.

Students rise up because they have to. Whether existing organizations are strong enough to intervene and give direction to these struggles differs from campus to campus. This is *the* challenge for traditional student formations. The recent protests pose a problem of leadership for traditional formations. I do not think that there can be some fundamentally new, significant force that can come up or hijack these organizations. What is crucial is how an organization manages a crisis and guides the process because, unfortunately, some of these actions degenerate, if there is no organizational form to give them a sense of direction—the events at TUT are an example of this degeneration, with students burning buildings and so on. This kind of action allows the focus to shift from the real issues. So the critical role of traditional student organizations remains clear.

While the protests at Wits and TUT did, in their initial stages, reflect the possibilities for radical student activism outside of the sanitized and constrained space of the traditional student movement, traditional student formations and institutional administrations worked swiftly to contain these eruptions by offering individual solutions to students around the problems of student funding. In the absence of any alternative forms of representation or consistent voices from the student body, SASCO and traditional student representative structures have provided form and tangibility to these campaigns. In both cases, individual SASCO members participated in and led some of the actions on the campuses, even though SASCO as an organization did not have any role in these actions. This suggests that students, including some within the student movement, continue to provide the radical potentialities and subjectivities necessary for change in society. However, the realization of these potentials lies perhaps no longer within or through the traditional organized formations of the student movement.

Notes

1. After the banning of SASO in 1977, the Azanian Students' Organisation (AZASO) was formed in 1981 representing the coming together of all Black Student Representative Councils (SRCs). While AZASO was closely aligned to the black consciousness tradition during its early years, it slowly became more influenced by the followers of the Freedom Charter and the traditions of the African National Congress (ANC). In the late 1980s AZASO reflected this change in its name, which became the South African National Students' Congress (SANSCO). Other student formations, such as the Azanian Students' Congress (AZASCO) and the Pan-African Students' Organisation (PASO) also emerged, but represented much smaller constituencies. While there were several differences that played themselves out between the different student political formations, this article will focus on the evolution of debates within the largest student political formation, SANSCO (which later becomes SASCO), as it is reflective of those debates that happened around neoliberalism within the ANC alliance, and thus contributed

to the changes that happened within large parts of the student movement. For the most part, where SANSCO and SASCO have been critical of the ANC government, other student political formations have been in agreement and often formed alliances around specific issues at a national level. Where this article makes use of the term "student movement" then, it refers specifically to those students organized under the banner of SANSCO and later SASCO.

2. Thami Ncokwane, Research & Policy Co-ordinator, SASCO National Office, interview, 2004.
3. SASCO, *The Size and Shape of Transformation (SPOT)* (2000), p. 3.
4. Kenneth Creamer, *The Student: Journal of SASCO* (April 1994), pp. 11–12.
5. Shape and Size of Higher Education Task Team, Council on Higher Education, *Towards a New Higher Education Landscape: Meeting the Equity, Quality and Social Development Imperatives of South Africa in the 21st Century*, http://education.pwv.gov.za/DoE_Sites/Higher_Education /CHE/CHE_Report30June2000.htm
6. *Ibid.*
7. Thami Ncokwane, SASCO, interview, 2004.
8. *Ibid.*
9. *Ibid.*
10. The theory of the National Democratic Revolution (NDR) refers to the belief held by the Congress movement that South Africa suffered from Colonialism of a Special Type (CST), in which race was used as a specific form of exploitation in apartheid society, necessitating a struggle conceived of in two stages—a struggle for national democracy in which the question of race would be addressed, and a "second stage" in which problems of an economic nature would be addressed. The NDR has been used to argue for time and patience to be given to the current phase in which the alliance finds itself, that of democratic governance (and black economic empowerment).Within SASCO, it became a disciplining tool as it allowed people to argue that any view critical of the ANC was working against the interests of the NDR and therefore "counter-revolutionary."

Part Two

Student and Worker Struggles at Three Universities in Post-Apartheid South Africa

The Struggle for a Better Education for All—UDW, 1995–2003

Fazel Khan

The former University of Durban-Westville (UDW), merged with the former University of Natal to become the University of KwaZulu-Natal in 2004, has a rich history of struggle. UDW was set up by the apartheid state as an "Indian" university but, consequent to staff, student, and worker struggles, the student body was deracialized in the 1980s and access was won for poor students. By the time of the merger UDW was the university for the poor. UDW was also the site of some longstanding and very interesting activism around curricula and relations with communities and social movements. However, UDW's history is multiple and conflicted and should not all be valorized. On the contrary, it includes strands of accommodation with apartheid, neoliberalism, and repressive managements as well as anti-African racism. But the best of UDW's history—the willingness to think critically, to fight domination, to build non-racialism and to forge worker, academic and student alliances—has never been written. In fact, in so far as these aspects of UDW have been written, it has been in the popular press where the campus's radical culture has been widely presented through a racist lens as an anarchic, violent, and dangerous insurgency.[1] This short article seeks to provide a very rough outline of the recent history of resistance and repression.

In our tenth year of democracy, celebrated with much stage-managed pomp, it would seem strange to the class of 1976 that their ideals about equal educational opportunities have been taken up by the new university administration, dusted off and given an entirely new spin. Equality might be ritually invoked but the real project is now about becoming "world class" which really means accelerating the process of commodification in the interest of local elites and against the interests of ordinary South Africans. Post-apartheid staff and student struggles at the former UDW bear a remarkable resemblance to those waged in other part of the continent and documented by the Committee for Academic Freedom in Africa.[2]

The astonishing shift toward the right in the ANC's government's economic policies, epitomized by Growth Employment and Redistribution (GEAR), has been at the core of recent staff and student discontent at the Westville campus of UKZN. This home-grown structural adjustment policy, implemented in 1996 without consultation, has resulted in a marked increase in both poverty and inequality. This has profoundly affected the university workers and students, the majority of who come from poorer communities.

I first came to the then UDW over ten years ago. It was the dawn of a new era. My generation was filled with hope we were going to transform our society and bridge the inequalities that I grew up seeing in a working class section of Chatsworth township. It was a "brave new world." But with all the euphoria at the prospect of building a new society there was, sadly, very little questioning of how our hopes would intersect with reality. We have paid a heavy price for our faith in the inevitability of positive change.

During apartheid our struggle had been clear. We were fighting a clear enemy—Afrikaner nationalism and its black collaborators. We all knew who the enemy was—they were overtly different from us and so our slogans were simple. *Shaya maBhunu* (attack the Boers) and *Mayibuye iAfrika* (Come back Africa). These were still the feelings that pervaded the university community in 1994. We really believed that black control of the university would realize our dream of building a critical university for the poor.

However in 1995, worrying rumors began to circulate about the need for greater "efficiency" at UDW. MANCO (the acronym for the UDW Management Committee) proposed to restructure the security and catering departments by retrenching staff—staff that were mostly African and therefore most vulnerable in a campus with a strong current of Indian nationalism. At the same time, the acting rector, Dr. Marcus Balintulo (the university's first African rector), published guidelines for registration of students for the 1996 academic year which stipulated that a registration fee of R2,300 was to be paid by all students before they could register. Students had disrupted a June 1995 graduation ceremony with chants of "we are hungry." *The Varsity Voice* (the official MANCO newsletter) of June 1995 carried the headlines "Hostel Students Gatecrash Graduation" and "UDW Anarchists Strike Again." Legitimate student concerns were seen as the workings of a few extremists wreaking havoc—similar to how George Bush sees the protests in Iraq. Students explained that they could not afford the exorbitant meal prices because after settling accommodation fees little was left over to buy food. MANCO did not respond to their concerns, although many students were chronically hungry.

Matters came to a head at beginning of 1996, when the management decided to go ahead with what they now quite openly called the privatization of security. Staff at the Campus Protection Service were to be retrenched and a private, external security firm contracted to do their work. MANCO sought to legitimate this in the name of the virtues of "cost-saving." Critiques pointed out that the retrenched workers were only paid a paltry sum of R210 a week and were hardly a major drain on resources.

Students knew that that increasingly harsh management demands around fee prices and payment schedules were placing their dream of university education under threat. Large numbers of staff, organized in the Combined Staff Association (COMSA), were facing retrenchment. Staff and students united in opposition to Balintulo and the commodification of the campus. The man who melded these two groups into a formidably cohesive fighting force was Ashwin Desai, a sociology lecturer, anti-apartheid activist, public intellectual, trade unionist, and president of COMSA.

The campus revolution of 1996 started, like all political upheavals, with a surprise incident that ignited popular passions. In February 1996 thirty-two workers were poisoned by toxic solvents that they were using in cleaning one of the residences. They had been working without supervision and had not been provided with appropriate protective clothing. MANCO was accused of gross negligence. It refused to take responsibility for the incident and the workers were ordered to continue working as before. Students passed a vote of no confidence in MANCO. COMSA followed suit. But COMSA's grievances were also linked to the management's general shift to neoliberal policies most notably the privatization of services and the deregistration of students with debts for fees. A class boycott and workers' strike was called for and heeded by members of both groups. Management found itself in the untenable position of fighting both workers and students. The workers and students stood united in their struggle for better conditions despite all kinds of intimidation and attempts to sow divisions. They had broken new ground—demonstrations had always assumed that apartheid and white managers were the common enemy—and now staff and students were united, two years after the fall of apartheid, in a militant struggle against a black management.

At a combined open-air mass meeting it was resolved that MANCO be marched out of campus and that the campus be managed democratically by staff and students. Later a stakeholder meeting decided to barricade the administration building to protest MANCO's arrogance. The next morning a human chain was formed around the administration building and MANCO was marched off campus.

MANCO called in the state in the form of the riot police as well as a private security firm called Combat Force which was owned by Norman Reeves, a former Rhodesian Selous Scout and member of the white supremacist Afrikaner Weerstand Beweging (AWB) to quell the uprising. The protests were finally subdued during the infamous "battle of the boom gate" at the eastern boom gate that opens into Varsity Drive. There, workers and students met a formidable force and were assaulted and shot at with rubber bullets. Many were hurt, some hospitalized. MANCO was then able to return to a campus. The campus was closed for two weeks.

In the weeks that followed, scapegoats had to be found and MANCO, like all able bureaucrats, found them in the likes of Desai and Evan Mantzaris, another COMSA leader. The student leadership was spared in what seemed to be an attempt to present the popular insurrection as the work of a few radical academics. This was a strategic mistake by management that would haunt them in later years as student militancy continued long after academic and worker militancy was crippled.

A commission was appointed by the then-Deputy President Thabo Mbeki to investigate the cause and likely solution to the UDW "disturbances." Called the Gautschi Commission it worked efficiently spewing out of hundreds of pages of documents, spending millions of rands, identifying scapegoats and suggesting solutions around access and job security that were, ironically, more or less what the protesters had been advocating. Some of its well-funded findings reeked of the bizarre. For example the young COMSA organizer, Heinrich Bomke, who happened to have a German name was identified as a Stasi agent (seven years after the fall of the Berlin Wall!). Most of the commission's recommendations were never implemented, but Desai was declared *persona non grata* and the battle to reinstate him continues. In 2004 he is certainly the most world-renowned intellectual writing in Durban but he continues to be excluded from university employment.

The following year, 1997, was, possibly due to the hangover from the previous year, largely uneventful. COMSA's more outspoken leaders had been suspended and the union was entangled in a legal quagmire. Thus COMSA's days as a viable and radical trade union, had ended. The only remaining centre of resistance to MANCO's undemocratic decision-making process was the Student's Representative Council (SRC). This period saw the rise of *Taifa La Wato*, a radical student organization that pursued a leftwing Pan-African agenda. It had tremendous appeal to students who had become disillusioned with the ANC aligned SASCO's (South African Students Congress) blind allegiance to GEAR policies. Started by the poet-cum-academic and former veteran of the liberation camps Professor Pitika Ntuli, this organization of progressive students sought to challenge "politics as usual." Under the fiery leadership of Dumisani Ncgobo the group won the SRC elections in 1997. Management responded with obvious unease and seemed anxious that 1998 was going to be a difficult year.

Early in 1998 rumors of a new round of financial exclusions began circulating. Students were asked, again, to pay the exorbitant R2,300 that many could not afford, however much their families sacrificed. Professor Mapule Ramashala was appointed as the new vice chancellor on May 9 in the presence of Deputy President Mbeki—a sign that she had government's support to continue the restructuring process at the university. Prof. Ramashala promised to improve the library, the residences and the lecture halls. However, in her explanation of her "new vision" she made no mention of the ever-increasing registration fee requirements. The student leadership was concerned about the fast dwindling numbers of enrolled students. There were already three thousand fewer students enrolled than in 1995.

In 1998, students set up a newspaper, *Akofena*, to push for freer news on the UDW political terrain. As a member of the editorial staff and a close comrade of the SRC, I was privileged to witness the events of '98 close up. The crux of the matter was again linked to the ANC's structural adjustment program that demanded that institutions cut down student debts and rein in expenditure. So Ramashala, the loyal hired gun decided to raise student fees. The student leadership protested, arguing that disadvantaged students had a right to an education. The vice chancellor was unmoved and the SRC declared a class boycott. During one of the numerous meetings with her, the student leadership refused to leave the administration venue where negotiations were taking place and MANCO called in the police to arrest them. The students were taken to jail and charged with loitering. On release they called for and began a hunger strike that galvanized the nation to the extent that it was discussed in the national parliament. Management eventually agreed to their demands, but it was a war that would not have been necessary had compassion prevailed from the onset.

The same problem of financial exclusions returned two years later. This time the SRC was dominated by SASCO, with Sandile Ndlovu as president. Some students could not afford to settle their debts and MANCO threatened to deregister them. Again there was a breakdown in talks between the management and students. COMSA made some show of solidarity with the students and announced a strike. But the strike was quickly called off when the union was informed that the strike would be illegal in terms of the Labour Act. COMSA was a spent force by then. No charismatic leaders had emerged after the expulsion of Desai and the union had not developed strategies for sustaining militancy in the absence of charismatic leadership.

With the June 2000 exams approaching, the students boycotted classes and demanded an end to financial exclusions. MANCO panicked and called in the police on May 16. The events of that crisp autumn afternoon tarnished UDW forever. A student, Michael Makhabane, was shot dead at point blank range with a shotgun as students fled the rubber bullets of the Public Order Policing Unit.[3] The ANC-aligned editor of the *Daily News*, Kaizer Nyatsumba, effectively endorsed the killing and there has never been an arrest or an apology.

The university was closed for two weeks to allow tempers to cool down. A commission of enquiry into the death of Makhabane was opened but no one has seen its findings to this day. Management heeded the students' demands and counseling for needy students was instituted which meant that students were assessed on a case-by-case basis and "deserving students" with debt were not excluded. Makhabane's death was a huge price to pay. No student had ever died on campus during the often-violent struggles against apartheid. *Hambe kahle, mfowethu* (Farewell, comrade).

Management did not dare go on the offensive in the following year. But that year saw a marked change in the political terrain due the death of the traditional left-wing student organizations and the beginning of the rise of the Socialist Student Movement (SSM). AZASCO (Azanian Student Congess) bled through a loss of good leadership and became a skeleton of its former self. The policies of PASMA (Pan-Africanist Student Movement of Azania) lost their popular appeal to students because they felt they had become obsolete. So did *Taifa La Wato*. It was a year when politics had degenerated to such an extent that candidates campaigning for SRC would promise more parties for students or buy beer to obtain votes. The political vacuum was filled by a small group of dedicated academics that argued that the real causes of the problems that had plagued post-apartheid UDW were not solely due to the personalities of management figures but included deeper structural forces. A considerable effort was made to point out the evils of globalization and to develop a new political vocabulary.

2001 saw another turning point in UDW politics when local community struggles against neoliberalism (especially struggles against evictions and water and electricity disconnections) took center stage. Previously staff and students had united in a common effort to defeat management. But in that year the entire global financial system was widely seen for what it was. It was a great year for noble protests. Staff, including Richard Pithouse and Pravasan Pillay, organized a march of 700 staff and students to the Merck Pharmaceutical company offices to demand access to affordable HIV/AIDS drugs for all.[4] Staff and students also worked with communities to protest against the commodification of water and made a major contribution to the national campaign for a ten rand flat rate. Staff and students (led by the SSM) also played a key role took part in antiwar demonstrations protesting against the US attack on Afghanistan. The SSM also organized a very large march on the offices of the Internal Complaints Directorate on the anniversary of the murder of Michael Makhabane to demand the arrest of the police officer responsible. To this day there has been no arrest.

This was also the year in which academics, workers and students united to propose a motion of no confidence in the vice chancellor, Prof. Ramashala, in the Senate. The motion was passed with overwhelming support. It accused the vice chancellor of an authoritarian management style and held her accountable for a range of devastating attacks on the academic life of the university including the sudden closing down of a number of departments (e.g., Fine Art and Music) because "they were not profitable." Ramashala and the state ignored the motion of no confidence. But at the end of 2002 Ramashala, a supporter of Thabo Mbeki's AIDS denialism who had unsuccessfully sought to ban the Treatment Action Campaign from the campus, was given the vice chancellorship of the Medical University of South Africa.

The appointment of Dr. Saths Cooper in 2003 ushered in a new epoch in UDW's history. With a year's mandate to gear the university for its coming merger with University of Natal, he changed the prevailing political landscape by soothing the animosity that existed between management on one side and staff and students on the other. The students and staff had always claimed that MANCO's autocratic management style was to blame for the past troubles at the institution. Contrary to his predecessors, Dr. Cooper encouraged the full participation of all the stakeholders in decision making. Staff unions and the SRC were to be consulted on all crucial decisions. Dr. Cooper even went as far as hosting open consultative meetings in UDW's major catchments areas—the working-class townships of Chatsworth, KwaMashu, and Umlazi. His stated aim was to consult parents and the community on the coming merger because he believed that a university's purpose should be to serve the society rather than, as in the neoliberal model, the other way around.

Cooper simplified the cumbersome UDW bureaucracy replacing some executives the previous VC had appointed due to political expediency rather than on qualification and experience. Many of these senior executives left or were reassigned to other posts. Next, the rampant corruption that had afflicted the student leadership was targeted. Ramashala, like all authoritarian managers, had always looked the other way on student governance issues. However, Cooper was having none of it. He immediately suspended and later expelled the Secretary General of the SRC, Muzi Madondo, on bribery charges that were upheld in a disciplinary hearing.

It was widely felt that Dr. Cooper's Black Consciousness Movement credentials helped him understand the plight of poor black students. In his first two months in office he simplified the financial counseling process thus making it easier for needy students to register. A record 11,700 students registered at the beginning of the year. It was the highest student enrollment in years. The Financial Aid Bureau applications were sped up to help students without funds to continue studying. A new residence was also hired to cater for the increased intake. The new Vice Chancellor rescinded Ashwin Desai's seven-year ban from the campus thus enabling the exiled former COMSA leader to present a memorable standing-room-only lecture.

It was also the year that saw the resurgence of the dormant COMSA. The unions had been silenced after the "battle of the boom gate" in 1996 when its leaders, including Desai, were suspended or expelled. The issue this time was job security as the institution faced the imminent merger that, although dressed up in the language of redress, was clearly a neoliberal cost-cutting exercise. For years the university had employed many workers and lecturers on one-year contracts. Cooper understood their grievances and many staff finally received permanency.

Student struggles took a back seat. After Madondo's expulsion, the freezing of tuition fees and the easier counseling process, all rallying points had been addressed and few could find fault with Cooper. There were only minor protests from an insignificant minority of conservative academics that had no popular appeal.

But notwithstanding all this progress, Cooper's populism had a dangerous side. He was prone to the vanity that afflicts the mighty. His face would dominate almost every photo in *Way To Go*, the management's official newsletter. No function would be spared the smiling face of this man who even put his image on the rulers handed out to first-year students. Moreover his delivery of job security to staff and access to students was matched by extravagant attempts to embrace the government that included a scandalous award to the AIDS denialist minister of health, Manto Tshabalala-Msimang. Many have ascribed Cooper's populism to a campaign to be installed as the new vice chancellor of the merged university. But his one-year contract was not renewed and so speculation about his agenda remains just that.

Professor Magalaperu Makgoba was installed as the Interim Vice Chancellor when the universities were finally merged at the beginning of 2004. He was at pains to assure students that there would be no financial exclusion of students in the coming year. But one only has to look at the 540 students who were denied financial aid to find a hole in his claims. He later published a circular stating that poor students, who could not meet their financial obligations, were going to be deregistered. More seriously, fees for new students entering the university from 2005 onward are set at much higher levels than those of the previous University of Natal. This means that although former UDW students currently in the system are not being asked to pay the much higher rates of the former University of Natal, all new students will have to pay these rates. This amounts to a blanket exclusion of the poor from ever becoming students. The subordination of the campus to the market, the state, and donor agencies is proceeding rapidly. The University of KwaZulu-Natal will clearly be a university of the rich in terms of access and in terms of its intellectual production. But resistance, led by the Socialist Students' Movement with the support of a handful of academics, continues.

Notes

1. The fact that black editors and journalists continued where their white predecessors had left off does not mean the fears projected onto UDW ceased being anti-African.
2. CAFA's work has been an inspiration for anti-neoliberal activists at the former UDW.
3. For an account of the immediate aftermath of the murder see Richard Pithouse, *Michael Makhabane*
   http://www.ukzn.ac.za/ccs
4. For Pillay's account of the march see *The March on Merck*
   http://www.weareeverywhere.org

Neoliberalism, Bureaucracy, and Resistance at Wits University

James Pendlebury and Lucien van der Walt

Over the past five years, the management of the University of the Witwatersrand (Wits) has busied itself with a thoroughgoing neoliberal restructuring project. Under pressure from declining government subsidies, arising from the South African state's neoliberalism, and influenced by the "market university" model, Wits management has, enthusiastically introduced measures to "transform" the institution. The overall effects on support service workers, on working class students, and on a significant section of academic and administrative staff, have been negative. This article examines the restructuring process, some of its internal contradictions, and the resistance that it has evoked.

The Neoliberal Context

There has been a general pressure on all South Africa universities to restructure in the post-apartheid period. While the initial impetus for "transformation" was the pressure to deracialize the fractured higher education system the actual content of "transformation" has been decisively shaped by the global neoliberal restructuring of capitalism refracted through the international state system.

In this context, the ANC's class project—deracialization of capitalism through the state—has been welded to neoliberalism. The adoption of the Growth, Employment and Redistribution

(GEAR) macro-economic policy in 1996 marked not the start, but the culmination, of the party's shift away from the traditional nationalist advocacy of import-substitution-industrialization, a move from state capitalism to market capitalism. There are still minorities within the ANC wedded to the old thinking, but the dominant position regards private investment as the motor of the economy, economic liberalization as the fuel, and global competitiveness as the speedometer.

As a bourgeois party, the ANC regards neoliberalism as an unavoidable part of its class project; as a bourgeois nationalist party, however, the ANC has a particular commitment to the rapid expansion of the African fraction of the bourgeoisie. This contradiction can only be resolved through adapting neoliberalism to the ANC's project: African capital is to be given preferential access to state contracts, and to shares in privatized utilities (e.g., Telkom), and bailed out where necessary (e.g., Sun Air); the labor market will be deregulated everywhere except in the sphere of employment equity; state spending will be cut everywhere except where it provides opportunities for accumulation (e.g., arms deal).

Now, with welfare spending in 1996 constituting the largest single item of State expenditure, and education spending at nearly 7 percent of GDP, the ANC's project necessarily collides with demands from below for increased expenditure. In terms of the higher education sector, GEAR argues that there "is a need to contain expenditure through reductions in subsidization of the more expensive parts of the system and greater private sector involvement in higher education."[1] The commitment to the "creation of new South African higher education institutions based on the values and principles of non-racism and democracy" is thus coupled to a commitment to fiscal austerity and liberalization, arising in the first instance from the class nature of state policy. [2]

In addition to facilitating austerity, subsidy cuts have served as a disciplinary mechanism within higher education: given the highly decentralized nature of the sector, with key decision-making power residing at institutional level, and given the reliance of institutions on state funds for most income, subsidy levels and formulae remain the key instrument for sectoral reform. The 1997/98 Budget allocated R5.4 billion to tertiary education, representing an average funding level of 65.6 per cent, down from the 68 per cent level of the previous financial year.[3] Wits, for example, saw its subsidy decline by a third from 1995 to 2000.[4]

Wits and the Market University

Fiscal austerity placed great stress upon the fifteen technikons and twenty-one universities. However, government has stressed that "given the magnitude of our other priorities," public sector tertiary education could not and would not receive additional resources.[5] It has instead stressed two solutions. On the one hand, mergers and disestablishments would rationalize the public sector tertiary education institutions from thirty-six to twenty-one. On the other hand, the State has promoted a model of university marketization in tandem with budget cuts. There is a strong emphasis on the need to generate funds through more "fee-paying" students, these being generated by diversification in feeder constituencies and program offerings, with courses made more narrowly vocational; equally importantly, there is a stress upon being more responsive to "social" and "economic" needs in order to generate "third stream" funding.[6] "Third stream" funding refers largely to state and business contracts, and is distinct from traditional revenue streams: student fees and state subsidies.

This set of ideas has been widely adopted, especially when dressed up in the language of "mode 2" knowledge production. This argues that research must be simultaneously applied, transdisciplinary, and team-based, whilst based in, and funded by, different organizations.[7] This sounds rather impressive, but is hardly earthshaking: disciplines have always overlapped, academics have often worked in groups, and universities have long cooperated with other institutions. What is new about "mode 2" is the funding model: institutions must now emphasize "third stream" funding, obviously in competition with one another and with other institutions.

The effect of such approaches is that research becomes driven primarily by financial, as opposed to intellectual, concerns, and that the research process evolves by being of potential use to the ruling class, ensuring its direct subordination to capital and the state. Dressed in the language of "relevance" to "society," such research is, in fact, frequently secret, and typically private (producing copyrighted intellectual property), while having little positive public results of "relevance" to the needs of the working class.

This enclosure of the collective, potentially emancipatory project of "scientific knowledge" is central to the notion of the "market university" in which institutions are reconceptualized as producers of intellectual commodities. Priorities, procedures, research projects, workforces, and curricula are restructured along business lines with profitability a key criterion; strict cost recovery for services rendered to students and other "clients" is emphasized; and corporate management styles and hierarchies are introduced. It is to this model that Wits aspires.

The 1999 Wits Strategic Plan argued that the university must, given declining subsidies, compete for funding, staff, and students with other universities.[8] More and better (and, crucially, better-heeled) students had to be attracted to increase government subsidies. At the same time the university had to become more cost-conscious and less reliant upon state support. This meant that entirely new sources of funding had to be tapped—in particular, the government and corporate sponsorship and contracts.

Several conditions promoted the shift to a market model at Wits. First, neither the university management nor popular constituencies were able to halt the process of subsidy cuts inaugurated in 1996. This was despite a rare convergence between factions in management and activists—exemplified by the appearance of arch-conservative Vice Chancellor Robert Charlton at a public protest organized by the left-wing Wits Against Cuts, or WAC, in 1997. Defeat led many otherwise sympathetic academics to accept the inevitability of painful change. It strengthened the hand of ANC-linked "modernizers" in management in their ongoing struggle against Charlton's conservatives. These modernizers would play the key role in marketization from 1999: their public face was former academic lefty, Colin Bundy, appointed Vice Chancellor in 1997.

Secondly, student and staff groups were unable to develop a systematic program and oppositional movement to the neoliberal agenda at Wits. Confusion about the class nature of the ANC led many formations, particularly those associated with the Congress tradition, to go with the neoliberal flow. The national leadership of the South African Students' Congress (SASCO), publicly endorsed the cuts of 1996 and 1997 as "redistributive" in nature, and Wits SASCO shied away from initiatives such as the WAC.[9] The National Education Health and

Allied Workers Union (NEHAWU), by far the largest and most militant campus union, with a base amongst manual and menial workers, was also crippled by its ANC alignment. Alternative movements, on the other hand, were simply not strong enough to pose an alternative. Coupled to growing student apathy, and academics' cynicism, this shifted the balance of forces powerful in favor of management.

Wits Inc.

The argument for repositioning Wits as a market university was elaborated in a case for the "formation of a University company for optimization of revenue opportunities from intellectual property and from entrepreneurial activities," the promotion of "revenue-generating activities" and "opportunities for entrepreneurial approaches across the University."[10] An Income Generation Program (IGP) was launched with corporate sponsorship, as an explicit step towards redefining Wits, and was a vehicle to promote academic involvement in fund-raising.[11] At the same time "Wits Plus" was launched to introduce part-time classes.

In 2002, Wits Enterprise was launched, described on its web site as a "University-approved commercial company," "a business vehicle jointly owned by the University and the staff," which offers a "world of short courses, training, consulting, contract research, and intellectual property." According to Peter Bezuidenhout, Wits' Marketing and Business Development director, it is a "new entrepreneurial business venture," a "channel" between "the university and the eternal commercial world" with a "mandate" to "promote and innovatively manage increased income-generating opportunities that could follow from the effective capitalization of present and future intellectual property assets of the university and its staff."[12]

It is not so very important whether Wits Enterprise actually becomes the main "channel" for research commercialization. Even in 2001, according to then-Acting VC Loyiso Nongxa, 83 percent of Wits' research income was already "externally sourced" from "partners in commerce and industry, as well as the science councils" of the state.[13] The significance of this autonomous company resides in what it symbolizes (embrace of the market university) and what it promotes (the capitalist ethic of linking research to "income-generating opportunities" and the "capitalization of present and future intellectual property assets"). It may indeed, as Nongxa hopes, "accelerate external funding" through "identifying and leveraging the business opportunities for research,"[14] but a serious impact on organizational and occupational culture would be revolution enough.

Academic Restructuring

Wits' repositioning had important implications for the management hierarchy of command and surveillance, and for staff and students. In 1999, management established a Task Group on academic restructuring. On September 27, 1999, the Task Group took its recommendations to the University's Senate, where it argued for the rationalization of academic structures: the existing nine faculties would merge into six, each under the control of executive deans, and the ninety-nine academic departments would merge into forty schools, each subordinate to a faculty.

These proposals were subsequently adopted, with Senate noting, politely, that it was "probable" that the restructuring "could have staffing implications." Two days later, the University Council established an Academic Restructuring Review Committee to take the Task Group's recommendations forward. The committee's brief included reviewing the size of academic entities, and establishing "appropriate" staffing levels and staff: student ratios. This implied that "redundant" courses would be closed, "redundant" disciplines phased out, and "redundant" staff closed out: initial estimates set the number of academics likely to be retrenched at twenty-five.[15]

The September 1999 Council meeting decided that these recommendations would be implemented over three years. At faculty level, Academic Planning and Restructuring Committees would propose measures for implementing the restructuring, to be implemented by the new executive deanships. Justified as a means of promoting "multi-disciplinarity," the academic restructuring was, in fact, governed by the application of private sector "best practice" to the institution. In particular, it was underpinned by a drive to power.

Power, including control over budgets and appointments, would move from department to school. More importantly, power would move from school to faculty, where it would concentrate in the hands of executive deans, whose role is basically to act as middle managers in the envisaged Wits Inc. This centralization is part of a drive to increase surveillance, to link job security to management targets, and to replace the guild-like structures of collegial governance with private sector managerialism.

A parallel process took place at the central level: Council, largely a rubber-stamp in the past, now increasingly marginalized the Senate, representing mainly senior academics, as decisive a policy-making structure; within Council, power was in turn concentrated in the Senior Executive Team (SET). Established in 1999, SET was made up of the VC, the key deputy-VCs, and consulted closely with the chair of Council. For the first time, a professional director of finance was included in the executive: in "keeping with a worldwide trend, the University saw the need to appoint a business-oriented person in this post rather than an academic professor as in the past."[16]

The emphasis on mergers and auditing the "redundant" was rooted in a new concern with implementing "cost-centering" financial systems. The aim was to phase out cross-subsidization between faculties—in particular, the traditional transfers from management, law, commerce and engineering to arts and education. From late 1999 onwards, in-principle decisions were taken on this issue; staffing in each cost-centre would depend on the ability of that centre to stay within its budget and raise funds to meet shortfalls.

Centralization and cost-centering were coupled to an increasing concern with surveillance. Using instruments such as a performance appraisal system from 2001 onwards, faculties were able to closely monitor the performance of individual lecturers; further, by making an implicit links between performance appraisals and job security, and an explicit link between individual ratings in the performance appraisals and discretionary wage increases, management was able to train its staff to work harder. The language of "human resource management" permeated Wits academia: the performance appraisal system was described as a method to "reward good performance and to create a culture of performance management and staff development."[17]

Gutting Support Services

In 1999, Wits also embarked on a Support Services Review process, investigating options for restructuring services as diverse as building maintenance, transport and the library system. It also announced that academic and support service restructuring would be jointly managed as "Wits 2001."

Undertaken by consultants, the University Management Associates (UMA)—paid R4.5 million for their time—the review process was, on paper, open-ended and participatory. In practice, as a close reading of the review itself shows, the UMA systematically ignored the views of academic and support service staff in favor of complete outsourcing.[18]

The UMA's final report, completed in 2000, advocated outsourcing cleaning, catering, maintenance, grounds, and transport. This would, supposedly, save Wits about R30 million over five years (later this figure was raised to R68 million, no reasons given), greatly improve service levels, and bring in expert management. Two basic ideas underpinned the UMA recommendations: first, support services were not part of the "core business" of Wits, and wasted money better spent on the research and teaching "core"; second, outsourcing was always efficient and infinitely preferable to internal restructuring.

The UMA cynically added that the workers themselves would benefit from the "greater career opportunities, training and accreditation" and "a degree of employment stability" created by outsourcing. It had to admit, however, that there were "human resources implications" that would obviously impact upon "career opportunities." SET endorsed these recommendations, and championed the review in Council. Doubtless it knew outsourcing would also gut the membership of the troublesome local NEHAWU branch, revolutionizing labor relations. A draft document to potential contractors suggested, in addition, that

> The MC [Management Contractor] shall discourage its employees from participating in any industrial action. In the event that the MC's employees are guilty of participating in industrial action, the MC shall control its personnel, restore order or, if requested by the Client, remove them from the Client's premises.[19]

On 25 February 2000, the UMA recommendations were endorsed by Council, although transport was later moved from the firing line when it become obvious to even the laziest Council member that the UMA had no idea at all about Wits transport. In effect, 613 workers, roughly a quarter of Wits' total staff complement of 2377, would be retrenched on June 30, 2000, their places to be taken by cheap non-union contract workers.[20]

NEHAWU organized pickets and marches, and refused to endorse the voluntary severance packages and counseling that management offered. However, NEHAWU relied mainly on a legal challenge to the retrenchments; campaigning was an appendix only. Radicals within SASCO pushed the organization into demonstrations in February and June 2000, and activists assumed control of the Post-Graduate Association, an SRC-type structure.

Links between academic restructuring and support service restructuring also rendered a fair amount of academics sympathetic to the workers' cause, but most were frankly disinterested or hostile. A small "Concerned Academics Group" played an important role in publicizing Wits 2001, and wrote a scathing critique of the Support Services Review.[21]

From about March, a radical "Wits Crisis Committee," drawing in people from a range of structures, played the main role. International allies were found, and placed pressure and a spotlight on Bundy. Direct action was taken. In early July, the committee helped organize an occupation of Bundy's office on June 20.

On July 14, 2000, a crowd of retrenched workers—plus student and academic activists and supporters of the "Anti-Igoli 2002 Forum," which campaigned against municipal privatization initiatives—stormed the Great Hall at Wits, where Bundy and head of Johannesburg Metropolitan restructuring Kenny Fihla were due to conclude a high profile "Urban Futures" conference. Perhaps the most important outcome was helping lay the ground for the subsequent merger of the Committee and the Forum in July to form the Anti-Privatization Forum (APF).

After Wits 2001

Bundy initially lashed out against the disruption with interdicts against workers and students, and moves were made to discipline certain academics. Cooler heads, however, prevailed, and these proceedings were quietly withdrawn. Bundy resigned in September and left the country, and was replaced in May 2001 by the amiable but naïve Norma Reid, an outsider with little knowledge of the issues but with no principled objection to marketization. Even before formally assuming office Reid advocated "working with the business and commercial sectors in mutually advantageous schemes for wealth creation" and the "commercial exploitation of intellectual property."[22]

It is significant that the APF failed to maintain a real presence at Wits. A mood of defeat after the retrenchments, coupled with widespread apathy, led to a sharp drop in campus struggles. NEHAWU lost over half of its roughly 800 members, including experienced shop-stewards. While maybe 250 Wits workers were reemployed by the contractors, NEHAWU failed to make an attempt to organize outsourced workers, or to keep its unemployed members together as a pressure group. Its strategy remained centered on a protracted legal battle, with legal depositions replacing popular mobilizations.

Vocal union actions were never linked to an attempt to forcibly stop the retrenchments; after June 30, outsourcing was rarely on the agenda at NEHAWU meetings, and then only in relation to the court case. The case was finally settled out of court in early 2003: the details of the settlement remain obscure. The stress on legal action reflected, on the one hand, NEHAWU's statist politics, and, on the other, its refusal to draw links between the retrenchments and ANC policy. ANC speakers even attended a union meeting mere weeks after the retrenchments to canvass for votes; the workers were told that opposition leader Tony Leon was actually the villain behind Wits 2001.

The conditions and wages of the outsourced workers were, it must be stressed, dramatically worse than those previously experienced by workers in Wits employ: the wages of cleaning staff dropped from around R2227 per month, plus access to medical aid, pensions and loans, with bursaries for children, to R1200 per month, without benefits.[23] This was coupled with a dramatic increase in workload and a pervasive fear of victimization, which undermined unionization.

Wits saved money at the expense of its lowest paid staff— executive salaries were never subjected to the same logic of cost cutting—and academic centralization found its complement in union-breaking in the support services. Most academics remained apathetic, with some even hoping that support staff cuts would mean academic benefits. There were, indeed, wage increases in late 2000, but these must be weighed against pervasive insecurity, individualization, and demoralization.

Academic workloads increased sharply: posts were routinely frozen whilst student numbers increased dramatically, reaching an all-time high of 24, 473 in 2003, as did pressure to increase research productivity. "Outside" work, formerly regarded as an unholy vice distracting from real university work, was now formally transmuted into a glowing virtue, an example of entrepreneurial skill and "relevance" that counted heavily in the performance appraisal system.

The student movement also declined sharply. Wits activists in the APF, including most of the new body's media section, soon focused their energies off campus. As activists withdrew from SASCO, the organization moved sharply to the right, forming a close alliance with the ANC Youth League and focusing on SRC elections, with intent to oust the dominant "non-political" Independent Students' Alliance (ISA). In late 2003 SASCO/ ANCYL narrowly secured control of the SRC, but aside from Congress-style rhetorical radicalism, there has been very little change in actual SRC activities.

The tragedy is that the "enterprising" university has already generated a range of student grievances. Support service outsourcing has led to repeated complaints of worsening conditions in student residences, where numbers of cleaning staff have halved.[24] Undeterred, Wits has (quietly) announced its intention to outsource the development and management of entire student residences.[25]

Wits has also forged ahead with policies of cost-recovery, introducing upfront fees payments from 2001, with an upfront payment of R2000 due at registration, and the remainder to be paid by the middle of the year. This is more than a little difficult for black working class students: in the same way that prepaid electricity meters lead the poor to self-disconnect, high upfront fees lead the poor to exclude themselves from the university rather than accumulate debts; the upfront fees serve as an automatic mechanism to regulate the class composition of the student body.

Important initiatives on several fronts have, however, come from smaller more radical student formations, such as the broad-left Socialist Students' Movement (SSM) and Keep Left. Formed at the beginning of 2002 the SSM played a key role in attempts to organize the outsourced workers, and to establish a workers' support committee. Frustrated by the Municipality, Education, State, Health and Allied Workers (MESHAWU) union, many outsourced workers left to set up a committee of their own, organizing a series of protests and moving, possibly, to an independent union.

Bureaucracy and Neoliberalism

It should be clear from this account that there has been a general drive towards the reconstitution of Wits as a market or "enterprising" university. It should not be assumed, however, that this means that everything runs smoothly and quietly. Instead, the restructuring of Wits is filled with contradictions and instabilities, characterized by bad planning, and shaped by the traditional bumbling of the Wits bureaucracy.

The fate of Norma Reid exemplifies these issues. Within eighteen months of her appointment, Reid was asked to resign by Council or face an internal inquiry into her activities. In line with the new stress on centralization, Reid's supposed sins were never made public, and she was forced out by the end of 2002. Reid had, it seems, erred mainly by failing to work in concert with the SET to drive the Wits restructuring process forward; it lagged noticeably during her term. The Wits bureaucracy had continually slowed the restructuring process; Reid's indecisive approach removed any real pressure for change, with the result that the bureaucracy sprang back into its old patterns.

The effect of the Reid period was that Wits restructuring only regained momentum in late 2003. After Reid's exit, the VC post was hurriedly transferred to Nongxa, first as acting VC, and then as VC proper in September 2003. The appointment was carefully managed: a Wits 2001 loyalist, Nongxa was the only VC candidate shortlisted, and thus, the only one allowed to campaign; his appointment was a foregone conclusion. Clearly, the Council and SET wanted to avoid a repetition of the Reid fiasco. Nongxa has been feted as a heroic figure; his defining characteristic is, however, his loyalty to Wits 2001.

If the ability to stage-manage the election of the VC is indicative of the extent to which power has already been centralized, then, the Reid affair is equally indicative of the limits to which the new regime has been consolidated. Poor planning by management has also played its part. The rapid increase in student numbers generated increased subsidies, but management failed to compensate for the increased pressures arising from this "fee-farming." Academic posts were frozen at the very moment that student numbers grew to unprecedented levels. Increased teaching pressures on staff meant, in turn, that Wits' strategy of generating "third stream" income was undermined.

Meanwhile few lecture venues at Wits could cope with the huge increase in numbers, the library system was increasingly out-of-date, and a disastrously recurrent incompetence became characteristic of the student registration process. At the same time, the Financial Aid Office overspent by R30 million in an attempt to increase student numbers, generating a deficit that wiped out the revenues generated through increased student numbers and setting the ground for a new hysteria about impending financial crisis. [26]

In Conclusion

Wits is, in short, well on the way to reconstitution as a market university. However, the restructuring process has continually generated contradictions and antagonisms, and management has proved far from an omnipotent entity. There are thus spaces for resistance, spaces that can grow into a more substantial challenge to the university as currently configured. In 2004, there are already signs of increasing student mobilization, whilst the outsourced workers appear to have again begun to move towards unionism. Amongst academics, few would now defend the Wits 2001 plan. From such seeds, something substantial might yet grow.

Notes

1. Government of National Unity (GNU), *Growth, Employment and Redistribution: A Macro-Economic Strategy* (Pretoria: Government Printers, 1996), 6.1.
2. K. Asmal, "Speech by the Minister of Education, Professor Kader Asmal, During the Debate on the Higher Education Amendment Bill," National Council of Provinces, October 9, 2001.
3. South African Institute of Race Relations (SAIRR), *South Africa Survey 1997/98* (Johannesburg: SAIRR, 1998), p. 137
4. F. Barchiesi, "Lean and Very Mean: Restructuring Wits University," *Southern Africa Report*, 15: 4, (2000).
5. Asmal, "Speech by the Minister of Education."

6. Department of Education, "Education White Paper 3: A Program for the Transformation of Higher Education," *Government Gazette,* 386, no. 18207 (July 1997).
7. N. Cloete and J. Muller, "South African Higher Education Reform: what comes after post-colonialism?" mimeo, 1998.
8. University of the Witwatersrand (Wits), *Strategic Plan,* (Braamfontein, 1999).
9. See, for example, N. Nieftagodien, "Wits Against Cuts," *Debate,* no. 3 (1997).
10. Wits, *Strategic Plan.*
11. See Barchiesi, "Lean and Very Mean."
12. University of Witwatersrand, Wits Enterprise, http://www.enterprise.wits.ac.za/, (accessed February 25, 2004): 22.
13. University of the Witwatersrand, *Annual Report 2002,* p. 9.
14. *Ibid.*
15. L. van der Walt, "Penalizing the Workers," *The Sowetan,* June 12, 2000.
16. University of Witwatersrand, "Meet the VC's New Executive Team," Wits Alumni E-Mail Forum Newsletter, no. 29, http://www.wits.ac.za/alumni/news29.shtml (accessed March 6, 2003).
17. Wits, *Annual Report,* 20.
18. G. Adler, A. Bezuidenhout, S. Buhlungu, B. Kenny, R., Omar, G. Ruiters, and L. van der Walt, "The Wits University Support Services Review: A Critique," (May 2000).
19. *Ibid.*
20. van der Walt, "Penalizing the Workers."
21. Adler *et al,* "Wits University Support Services Review."
22. Quoted in L.van der Walt, D. Mokoena, and S. Shange, 2001, "Cleaned Out: Outsourcing at Wits University," *South African Labor Bulletin,* 5: 4, (2001), p. 58.
23. *Ibid.*
24. *Ibid.*
25. University of the Witwatersrand, "Call for Expressions of Interest," *Mail and Guardian,* January 16-22, 2004, p. 30.
26. M. Mnisi, "Finance Dismisses Bankruptcy Claims," *Wits Student,* 56:1, February 2004.

World Bank Thinking, World-class Institution, Denigrated Workers

Jonathan Grossman

> To build real People's Education workers must give
> guidance so as to make sure we do not end up with a new
> education system that remains trapped within capitalist
> ideology.
> —*Alec Erwin, 1985, then trade unionist, now Cabinet Minister*

Much analysis and commentary on World Bank thinking and
programs has correctly focused on the economic devastation that
they have historically promoted and caused. Critics have pointed
to "marketization" and "commodification" in higher education,
and their specific implications for universities.[1] More recent
analysis, taking account of the rhetorically restyled World Bank
emphasis on development to deal with poverty, has pointed,
correctly, to continuities with the politics and economics of the
Washington consensus.[2] Taking these critiques as established, I
will look at how World Bank thinking necessarily translates into
specific attacks against workers and their organizations at the
university.[3] I will then consider the impact this in turn has on the
political and social ethos of the institution. My focus is on the
University of Cape Town (UCT), but these issues are repeated
and confronted elsewhere.[4]

At a forum to discuss economic alternatives in 2003,
Mamphela Ramphele, a senior manager of the World Bank,
expressed her concern and disappointment because the Congress
of South African Trade Unions (COSATU) was doing so little to

challenge the ANC government. Trevor Ngwane, of the Gauteng Anti-Privatization Forum (APF), pointed out that, in her last managerial job in South Africa, she had driven through the cancellation of a recognition agreement with the trade union, the retrenchment of the majority of workers, and the effective decimation of the union at the site of her "core business." According to Ngwane, she responded, no doubt with pride, that she was "guilty as charged," and went on to explain that this had been done in order to benefit poor blacks.[5] The business involved was UCT, the poor blacks reputed to have reaped the benefits were students, and her management position was as UCT's Vice-Chancellor and Principal. She held this position between 1996 and 2000 before moving directly to the World Bank as one of four managing directors.

Ramphele was helpfully straightforward when she assessed her impact on UCT. Styling herself as an "innovator," she seemed to act in terms of a well-used handbook of World Bank thinking. It was her innovation, she declared, that UCT was meant to "run as a business committed to balancing its books." In the context of an elitist university within a grossly unequal society, she focused particularly vigorously on what she saw as a key problem:

> We had gross distortions in our salary and wage structures; in a nutshell, we overpaid at bottom level and underpaid at the top. We needed to review and rationalize our staffing structures and numbers to ensure we retained the best and eliminated "dead wood."[6]

Implementing this approach posed a problem. There was a well-established union with a partly progressive recognition agreement that organized the "overpaid" workers at the bottom level. "Balancing the books," as Ramphele planned, also threatened some academic jobs. In pursuing her agenda of wage reductions at the bottom and salary increases at the top, Ramphele was able to exploit the basis laid over previous years by the white liberal management of UCT. In 1991 Stuart Saunders, UCT's then Vice-Chancellor, addressed the issue of wages central to an aggressive strike:

> Members of the Transport and General Workers Union in pay classes 1, 2 and 3 are on strike at UCT. The university is always ready to negotiate and details of the salary and benefit offer have already been published. All I need to say is that the university's offer maintains our position as a leader

among employers. The minimum wage offered is R1,202 per month, plus a 13th cheque, plus free medical aid, plus a housing subsidy, plus other benefits.[7]

Saunders went on to invoke the argument of the innocent third party, which has become so central to anti-strike positions. While he was willing to concede that workers had the right to strike, students had the right to study without disruption. Come what may, the university would continue as normal. Within an increasingly socially prevalent human-rights discourse, the argument of non-disruption was smoothly elevated into a principle of protecting rights. Rights crucial to working class mobilization are simply reduced, in this view, to secondary and conditional rights. There is an effective veto given to those who enjoy the primary rights: the "innocent third party" includes the students and management; in other words, anyone, except the workers.

Under apartheid South Africa, UCT workers had been among the first to win a recognition agreement recognizing the right to strike without fear of dismissal. Workers at UCT had also been at the forefront of the struggle for some form of protection against retrenchments. The most they had been able to win, which was far in advance of workers at many other workplaces, was last-in-first-out (LIFO) across the board. However limited this protection in the recognition agreement, it stood in the way of plans to retrench and outsource. Management was unable, while the agreement stood, to target particular departments, sections, and units for closure and outsourcing. Their problem was compounded because it was precisely the units they wished to target where workers tended to have longer service, and therefore some protection through LIFO.

In its public relations, UCT portrays a record of struggle against apartheid and for human rights. However, no aspect of the recognition agreement of value to workers, or the development of the union was the result of liberal goodwill. There is a long history of organization, mobilization, and struggle behind the eventual decision of management to recognize the union. This history included a combination of worker action, student action, the broader social context of mobilization and action, and attempts to exploit liberal sensitivities. The Ramphele agenda required that some of these key gains of struggle, won in apartheid South Africa, should be reversed in post-apartheid South Africa. In 1998, two shop stewards were dismissed during a strike around wages. UCT management, which had been unable to stop repeated invasions of campus by apartheid police to attack protesting students, now used court injunctions to protect "normal functioning" and its "private property" from striking workers. The union refused to participate in negotiations with management until the shop stewards were reinstated. Under Ramphele's management, the university cancelled the recognition agreement because of a breach of "good faith" by the union. Freed from the historical constraints of that agreement, the university followed the "innovative" plan of retrenchment and outsourcing, in order to focus on "core business" and save money. At the time, Ramphele spoke of the decision as "extremely painful."[8] As with many painful decisions, the pain here was all imposed by those taking the decision on its victims.

In adopting vigorous anti-strike approaches and harsh measures against a union seeking to protect its members, Ramphele was aided by policies adopted by key leaders in the new ANC- led government. The elections of 1994 approached in the midst of probably the biggest strike wave ever in the public sector. Prominent ANC and Communist Party leaders called on workers to suspend action in the light of the elections. In February 1995, Mandela warned striking public sector workers that their disruption was embarrassing their government: "Mass action of any kind will not create resources the government does not have and will only serve to subvert the capacity of the government to serve the people."[9] If anti-strike arguments were made prevalent in general, this was particularly the case in relation to "education." Strikers could expect accusations of denying students the right to study, placing their own interests ahead of those of "the nation," harming the innocent in defense of their "privileges."

It would be possible to see Ramphele's approach simply as an act of union bashing. That was part of the reality. But from management's perspective, it was also inextricably tied into a stated vision of making UCT more accessible to poor black students, dealing with problems of gender inequality and inequity, and positioning the university as a "world class institution." The mission statement included the aims to "transcend the legacy of apartheid" and "to overcome all forms of oppression."[10] From management's perspective, measures against workers seeking to protect themselves were a necessary part of transformation at an apartheid institution. In this set of attacks against workers in the name of progressive social goals, there is a striking similarity with the movement between the Reconstruction and Development Program (RDP) of 1994 and the neo-liberal Growth, Employment and Redistribution Program (GEAR) of 1996. There is also an important lesson to be learnt in our assessment of "World Bank thinking."

When GEAR first appeared "from above," it took many progressive thinkers and activists inside and outside the ANC by surprise. They pointed to an apparent rupture between the progressive social goals of the RDP and the reactionary economic measures of GEAR.Under pressure from such quarters, the ANC leadership responded that RDP goals still remained and were in fact appended to the GEAR documents. GEAR was adopted, they argued, as the route to securing those goals. They could argue correctly that the goals of international competitiveness and the spirit of individual competitiveness were already embedded in the RDP. In similar fashion Ramphele was arguing that her "rightsizing measures" at UCT which involved tearing up the recognition agreement and retrenching the workers were necessary in order to promote UCT's progressive social goals.

We now have a partly restyled World Bank which is claiming much of its apparently progressive social goals in education.[11] We are bound to ask: what has changed of the steps to be taken to achieve those goals? In the midst of the apparently progressive goals, the signs of continuity with the basic values of the Washington consensus are there; in the practice of bosses' government after bosses' government in the capitalist global village, they are unmistakable. Education is for international competitiveness in the world market. Translated into individual terms, education is predicated on the development of individual competitiveness. If, as in stated policy, education has to be extended to those historically denied it, and focused particularly on reaching girls in poor countries, it also has to go together with the values of the capitalist market. Embedded in and infesting the apparently progressive social goals are the values of the capitalist market that undermine and prevent their achievement. Inextricably linked to the apparently progressive social goals are the anti-worker measures that are deemed necessary to reach them. In restyled as much as in "old" World Bank thinking, higher progressive goals demand such action. If unions have a role, it is in policing agreements reached by "social partners." One of the most direct critiques of the "new" World Bank agenda is based on the way in which it involved a direct attack against workers and their unions in the public sector internationally.[12]

If workers insist that their unions actively and effectively seek to protect them and promote their interests, those unions have to be smashed. Action by workers to resist this is deemed unpatriotic, and demonized as reactionary. It is deplored as driving away foreign investment, and bourgeois economic thinking can see no possibility of any progress without such investment. The ethic of individual competitiveness and the over-riding goal of international competitiveness justify and in fact demand that the lowest-paid be paid even less and the highest-paid receive even more. Action against workers and their unions is neither a regrettable necessity nor an "unintended consequence." It is made a goal to be pursued with vigor and determination even when initially justified in the name of higher, apparently progressive goals. All of this is necessary even if the educational site itself is not necessarily seen as having to generate a profit; even more so where it is actually also a site channeling profits through to private contractors.

The "dangers of a rampant and profane marketization and commodification of higher education" are perfectly visible to academics.[13] There is no shortage of warnings about the threatened consequence in everyday academic life: that "the moral and ethical considerations of how and what we teach and teach towards is ignored or becomes an afterthought"; nor of the need to ensure that "the political, social and intellectual life of our country will be not be banal, self-centered, and mired in greed or desperate attempts at simply survival."[14] No less visible are the practices that warrant and then disregard the warnings. Most commonly, the warnings are directed at aspects of academic work—what we teach, how we teach. But what about our own backyards? What does it mean for the life and work of a university if apparently progressive educational goals are necessarily linked to attacks against workers and their organizations? What does it do to a supposed ethos of critical social enquiry, and to the mission of "responsiveness and engagement" in a society based on deep structured social inequalities and injustices? What *has* it done at UCT?

Effects of the Ramphele Retrenchments

During the strike of 1991, Saunders said that the university was paying R1,200 per month— then well above the market rate. He pointed to additional benefits of medical aid, housing, transport, and other subsidies. Thirteen years later, after ten years of democracy, what has changed? Some retrenched workers are still unemployed. Workers doing the same work at UCT, now for the private contract companies, are paid R1,300 per month. The subsidies have all been removed. Given both fourteen years of inflation and the fact that they no longer get the benefits that Saunders boasted about, a dramatic reduction in income has been imposed on workers in the post-apartheid university. Part of the Ramphele mission has been achieved.

In 2002, workers from a contract cleaning company began a campaign of mobilization for a back dated pay increase. The sum involved was tiny—R266. However as a pamphlet at the time pointed out:

> Maybe that sounds like a little money to many of you. You are right. It is very little. But it is our money. And it is staying in the pockets of our bosses. When you are paid the peanuts we are paid, R266 matters very much. It is clothes for a child that must go to school; it is school fees; it is food for someone that is hungry; or medicine for someone that is sick. [15]

In 2003, student activists from TakeactionUCT conducted a series of interviews with cleaning workers. In interview after interview, as with meeting after meeting, workers repeat the same features of their lived experience of working for a contractor at UCT. Being a contract worker at UCT means living in poverty, insecurity, and debt. It means a workplace dominated by arbitrary decisions imposed by managements with no respect for workers' dignity. And it means a culture where workers are made to fear the consequences of exercising simple democratic rights, like voicing their complaints, protesting, organizing, and striking. However appalling wages and conditions were at companies before they won contracts from UCT, they were further squeezed by the bottom line thinking of UCT management.

Serious examination of any aspect of the problem at universities necessarily comes up against the issue of funding. Funding is in turn a reflection of dominant visions of what is or is not socially valuable. For as long as the definition of social value is in the hands of World Bank thinkers, it will, in effect, be absolutely bounded by that which is productive for profits. Campaigning for redress, reparations and solutions at the universities will undermine itself if it is caught up in the same value framework—being reduced in turn to the promotion of funding as investment in that which is deemed productive for profits. Amongst other things, our universities are infused with a deeply rooted competitive individualism, promoted at almost every point. As with all ideology, it is not merely ideology, but affirmed by a basis in lived experience. Erstwhile activists end up as rising university administrators. Trade union organizers end up as human resource managers. Erstwhile academic critics find themselves on committees which caution "realism" to remaining academic critics. There are workers who will work for starvation wages, forced to tolerate the intolerable because they are desperate. The elitist university survives and flourishes on more and more private funding and, at the same time, is systematically deprived of public funding. There is no real desperation here, just an increasing accommodation with whatever is necessary to get private funding.The ethos this promotes simply affirms the underlying ideology and practice. It is reflected in the physical path of a student at UCT, across the sports fields festooned with the banners of Old Mutual, past the statue of Cecil John Rhodes, into a lecture in the Nedbank room, and thence to the Oppenheimer Library.

In 2000 workers at the University of Witwatersrand faced the same retrenchment and outsourcing as had happened at UCT. An article for the UCT workers' newsletter in April 2000 asked:

> Is this meant to be a university which is contributing to building a better life for the poorest of the poor, or is it a university which wants to reward only the richest of the rich? Will our students leave here with an education that gives them respect for the people whose hands built this country, or will they leave with respect for people whose hands are only busy counting money? There are 241 workers at UCT and 600 workers at Wits who are going to say: "Don't listen to nice words anymore. Look at what they do. That is who they are."[16]

The vision of a very different kind of education was exemplified in COSATU education policy in the 1980s. This came in the midst of massive working class mobilization against employers and their apartheid regime. It was a time when COSATU had more of that critical approach whose demise Ramphele apparently deplores, but actually promoted. Amongst other things, "COSATU was critical of ruling class values, which they identified as racism, sexism, individualism, careerism, competitiveness, and elitism."[17] The World Social Forum sloganizes as part-analysis, part-program, part-dream that "another world is possible". There will be no socialist alternative to the brutality of the everyday of capitalism without the self-activity of millions of organized, mobilized workers in a collective movement of struggle. The ethos of a university that tramples on the lives and dignity of its workers does nothing at all to open up visions of hope of that other world. World Bank thinking fosters a vision of human rights in which the rights of workers are made secondary and conditional and thereby rendered effectively meaningless. Public sector funding is deployed to promote training in the values and practices of private sector profit accumulation and public sector cost recovery, commercialization and privatization. Its favored privatization and public-private partnership is a conduit for public funds and assets to end up fuelling private profit. Through the process, it further infests the already infested public sector in the capitalist state with the principles and practices of competitive sustainability and commercialization. The individual student faces a regime of more aggressive "cost recovery," cutthroat "performance evaluation," and debt that is being transferred from the institution to the individual. These most harshly affect the student without private means and earlier "good schooling". Striking or simply protesting workers are demonized to students as an obstacle in the way of their own advancement. What respect for ordinary workers can possibly surface and survive in this context?

Student and Academic Resistance?

Nevertheless, in 2004, student activists have gathered the support of an unprecedented number of students in a demanding changes and improvements for workers. But student numbers decline dramatically when there is action and more so when there is worker action. A minority of students struggles effectively to rise above the avalanche of individualizing, competitive, and essentially anti-working class pressures and practices. Many of the students arrive with the values embedded in that ideology and flourish within such a university ethos. There is nothing essentially new about it at UCT. What is new is the aggressive arrogance with which it is being promoted and the way in which it is being legitimated as that which is not only necessary but also the only way to promote apparently progressive social aims. Some students pick up the aggressive competitive individualism and try their best to emulate it. Others are troubled by it but denied anything around them suggesting qualitatively different alternatives. I am not here talking simply, or even primarily, of courses whose content challenges the sterility and hopelessness of the pervasive repetition of the orthodoxies of the capitalist market. Instead, I am highlighting the context imposed on students of a university that silences its own workers when they seek to deal with exploitation and oppression, and systematically denigrates them as a normal part of daily routine.

There have been some generally disregarded and often isolated academic objections to the situation imposed on workers. Academic objections to the outcome of World Bank thinking at one point are too often undermined when they are silent or supportive of World Bank thinking at another point. Couched in terms of narrow academic self-interest, an objection invokes part of the same basis on which economic and political attacks against workers are being justified. The reality is that any substantial academic objection to reactionary measures has been based on sustained worker resistance and sometimes also student resistance. The passivity of academics during the Ramphele years reflected the decline of student and worker mobilization as well as perceived threats to academics' own position. At the time of the worker retrenchments, one encountered a standard response to any suggestion of academic resistance: "Be careful, you are next." As with many academic jokes, there was little humor involved, but it spoke of a climate of fear, caution, self-censorship, passivity, and demoralization. Each of these is a devastation of any critical social enquiry or action directed at the "sacred cows" of the university itself. When the textbook Economics 101 package of retrenchment, outsourcing, and marketization has itself become a sacred cow of the university, not just of the broader society, then what scope are academics leaving for vigorous critical social engagement?

Academics often claim a particular expertise in debunking and getting to the analytical core of social realities. That is all well and good. Sometimes this ends up obfuscating what are simple political realities and clear political tasks. What has happened at UCT is wrong. Putting it right requires us to call it by its right name and to act to change it. Along the road, exposes and rigorous investigation are necessary and useful. But there is too much of a tendency for that to become the substitute, not part of the contribution. UCT, like other universities, has people who can write necessary and useful scholarly critiques of World Bank thinking and action. There are papers and policy documents and sometimes even petitions. There is scholarly work exposing the negative impact on "development"—yet some of that work emanates from offices cleaned by people who are forced deeper and deeper into a cycle of debt because of the wages they are paid. There is similarly scholarly work on the negative impact on health and safety. Yet it can emanate from offices cleaned by people who cannot afford basic health care and are forced to work in unsafe and unhealthy conditions. The workers who clean the office from which such critiques emanate are living the consequences of World Bank thinking everyday. But when the workers and students picket, march, or strike, they are almost completely on their own. Warnings about the dangers of marketization and commodification sometimes come at conferences and in papers and are then "put on hold" for a practice which ignores them until the next conference or paper. At UCT, the costs of this marketization and commodification in the daily lives of ordinary workers has been justified and in fact demanded as necessary to achieve progressive social goals— even to "adequately" pay the academics producing articles about it. Living with that contradiction and doing nothing about it is simply fuelling an ethos that promotes the problem in the first place.

A university following such a market-driven approach necessarily becomes increasingly impoverished as a centre of critical social enquiry, even more so as a site mobilizing and deploying resources to the service of the ordinary worker. A moment's glance at what has happened to a group of the poorest black people involved—the workers—shows the real nature of concern. Similarly, tracking a poor black student of working class background through a university based on such an ethos would show how the student also becomes the social, emotional and political victim. It is an ethos which requires that you deny the knowledge and integrity of your own working-class background, learn the market morality of profit before all else, and prepare yourself to go out into the "real world" to help other poor blacks by becoming "filthy rich,"[18] retrenching workers, driving down wages and conditions, outsourcing, and smashing unions. Little wonder that the personification and "innovator" of all of this at UCT should find herself in the senior management of the World Bank.

Notes

1. L. Orr, "Globalisation and Universities: Towards the 'Market University'?," *Social Dynamics* 23 (1) (1997), pp. 42-67.
2. See C. Soudien, "Education in the Network Age: Globalization, Development and the World Bank," *International Journal of Education Development* 22 (2002), pp. 439–50; and Bretton Woods Project.
http://www.brettonwoodsproject/.
3. See L. van der Walt, C. Bolsman, B. Johnson, and L Martin, "The Outsourced University: A Survey of the Rise of Support Service Outsourcing in Public Sector Higher Education in South Africa and its Effects on Workers and Trade Unions, 1994–2001," *Sociology of Work Project*. University of the Witwatersrand, Johannesburg (2002).
4. See E. Bertelsen, "The Real Transformation: The Marketisation of Higher Education," *Social Dynamics* 24 (2) (1998), pp.130–58.
5. Personal conversation.
6. *Monday Paper,* September 20, 1999.
7. Letter to staff, September 1991.
8. *Monday Paper,* November 25, 1998.
9. *Argus,* February 17, 1995.
10. See http://www.uct.ac.za/.
11. See World Bank, *Education Sector Strategy.* (Washington, DC: The International Bank for Reconstruction and Development/The World Bank, 1999).
12. Bretton Woods Project, November 17, 2003.
13. S. Badat, "Introduction" in *Re-inserting the "Public Good" into Higher Education Transformation* (Pretoria: Council on Higher Education, 2001), p. 2.
14. *Ibid.* p. 3.
15. UCT Workers Support Committee pamphlet, November 2002.
16. The newsletter was not published.

17. S. Andrew, *Cosatu's Policy on Worker Education, 1985–1992.* Masters dissertation, University of Cape Town (2003), p. 71.

18. The now famous phrase of a current Minister.

Part Three

Post-Apartheid Disciplines

Is African Studies at UCT a New Home for Bantu Education?

Mahmood Mamdani

Is African Studies at UCT a New Home for Bantu Education?

I was appointed as the A. C. Jordan Professor of African Studies at the University of Cape Town in September of 1996, and then as director of its Centre for African Studies in early 1997. I spent my first year startled that I had only one colleague and no students in the social sciences. I wondered to whom I was supposed to profess. When I shared this thought with a senior administrator, suggesting that surely the decision to appoint a professor of African Studies must have been taken as part of a larger decision to create a core faculty in African Studies, he did not disagree, but advised me to wait until one of the people in the larger departments in Arts either died or retired and then press for more intellectual resources. The thought did occur to me that I may have been hired as an advertisement, a mascot for the Centre for African Studies, and that I should not take myself too seriously. But I shoved this thought out of my mind as soon as I became conscious of it.

The Centre, I realized, was mainly an extracurricular affair. I could and did organize conferences where South African intellectuals could meet counterparts from the equatorial African academy, as in March and October of 1997, but this left untouched the key problem of the Centre: that it was totally marginal to the real work of the university—teaching and research.

Then came an opportunity that I thought would surely provide me a way out of this dilemma. It was October 1997, and by now I was over a year old at UCT. I was approached by the assistant dean of the Faculty of Social Sciences and Humanities, Associate Professor Charles Wanamaker from the Department of Religious Studies, who informed me that the faculty was taking a bold new step to design a foundation semester, which would be compulsory for all entering social science students. The core of the foundation semester would be a course on "Africa." He requested that I design the syllabus for this course. It seemed a golden opportunity to step out of extracurricular preoccupations and get involved in the mainstream of social science teaching. I decided to seize it with both hands.

I put one request before the assistant dean at the outset. I said that even though I considered myself a historically informed social scientist, I would need the help of a historian to do the work well. I added that though UCT had a large Department of History—I think it had fourteen faculty members in established posts—it had only one person whose research focus was outside of southern Africa. That was Dr. Shamil Jeppie, whose research interest was Sudan. I concluded that I would need to get the assistance of a historian from the University of Western Cape, and that this person would have to be paid, the Deputy Dean agreed. I went on to secure the support of Dr. Ibrahim Abdullah as a consultant, requesting that he provide me with bibliographical assistance, directing my reading on issues where I felt particularly weak. And then I began work, on average six hours a day for six days a week, with a passion that I would say I had not experienced since I left Kampala for Cape Town in late 1996.

In mid-October 1997, I presented a draft outline, called "Problematizing Africa" to the relevant faculty committee, and followed with a revised outline on October 30. With the acceptance of the outline, I was asked to come up with appropriate readings and to liaise with a working group of three (Digby Warren, Mugsie Spiegel, Johann Graaff) for purposes of implementation. The tussle that followed with the working group and the deputy dean was one for which I was totally unprepared. As it unraveled, it highlighted issues that I think go beyond my personal predicament: the relationship between the defense of academic freedom and the pursuit of academic excellence, administrative decision-making in academic affairs, and the relationship of pedagogy to content. It is because I believe these issues to be of general concern that I have decided to elaborate them before presenting my review of the substitute course that was put together under the leadership of the same team.

Academic Freedom and Academic Excellence

When I met the working group, on the November 14, the chair (Digby Warren) began the meeting by distributing the results of a poll. On the sheet I was given were listed the eight section titles from my course outline. Every discipline in the faculty was invited to indicate whether they considered each section title "very important," "of some importance" or "of less importance." The poll showed that most departments considered the first four sections of the course to be "of less importance" and the remaining four to be "very important." I was asked to revise the syllabus in light of this result. I asked whether this was the procedure normally followed for every new course introduced in the faculty or whether it had been designed especially for my benefit. I was told that it had been designed especially for my benefit, since this was to be a faculty-wide course.

I was, frankly, amazed. I pointed out that whereas a poll can give us facts, it cannot give us the interpretation of facts; the poll could be read as indicating either deficiencies in the proposed course or it could illuminate something about the respondents themselves. Was it not illuminating, I asked, that the respondents seemed to think it "of less importance" to teach the history of Africa before colonialism?

Among those in the working group, Dr. Spiegel of the Department of Social Anthropology objected; social science, he said, was about modernity, and history had no place in it. I said he must be the first anthropologist I had met who seemed to have embraced modernity as a faith. Dr. Graaff of the Department of Sociology joined in and said that he wanted to teach Marx's notion of class and he could not do this with a section on slavery, and that he needed a focus on modern society to do this. I doubted that I had ever met an ahistorical Marxist in my life, and I said so. The meeting closed with the chair asking me to prepare the tutorial readings so the full course could be ready before I left town on December 4. I agreed.

Administrative Decision-Making

Sadly, the very day I finished this task, but before I could communicate the final results of my labor to the faculty, I received a letter from the deputy dean formally suspending me from the course for 1998. He wrote that I needed more time to complete the course design, a bit of reasoning that made no sense to me since I had just finished the course. Even more perplexing was information casually included in the letter: that the faculty intended to go ahead with the course in 1998 as "an interim arrangement." I realized that, while I was being asked to take a year's sabbatical, another group was being invited to prepare a substitute course with haste. Was I wrong to take this as a vote of no confidence in my competence as professor of African Studies?

I left Cape Town two days later for Kampala, but before doing so, I protested this decision by administrative fiat. The deputy dean remained silent, however, and stayed so for the next three months. The institution remained complacent while senior administrators passed the buck back and forth. The dean of the faculty said the matter should really be handled by the chair of the Board of African Studies (BOAS) since the Centre for African Studies was an inter-faculty unit, and the chair of BOAS regretted he could not interfere in an internal faculty matter.

On my return, I was called in by the Vice Chancellor (February 10, 1998) who suggested a roundtable of all parties concerned—a suggestion her deputies, Professors Gevers and West, modified in a meeting (February 26), recommending a Mediation Commission / Commission of Inquiry, instead. When another two weeks went by without any sign of action, I decided to call a one-person strike. "Faced with a complacent institutional response, and a disabling institutional environment," I wrote members of BOAS and the university authorities on March 9, "I have no choice but to suspend all institutional involvement until the subject of my protest has been effectively addressed."

Pedagogy and Content

This is when the institutional wheels began to turn. The roundtable was held two days later, on March 11. Deputy Dean Wanamaker said that, faced with a difference between the working group and myself, he had decided "to take the soft option" and suspend me. He said I did not seem to realize that the choice of Africa as subject matter for the course was "purely arbitrary," that "the real point of the course was to teach students learning skills." Since they had to peg this to some subject matter, "that subject matter could just as easily have been Cape Town or South Africa," possibilities they had considered earlier.

My point of view could not have been more different. I argued that no matter what the subject matter—Cape Town, South Africa, or Africa—once it had been chosen, it was the obligation of those with expertise in the field to ensure that concern with pedagogy not become an excuse to teach substandard content. He said he thought this was really a cultural problem. I pointed out that he would not get away with this statement in the American academy, even in the American South, where I understood he came from. I said I thought they had a word for this.

There followed two formal, printed apologies, one from the dean and the other from the deputy dean, circulated at the faculty board meeting of March 19. I circulated a statement that "warmly welcome(d)" the apologies, but with two reservations, both on grounds that the apologies did not identify the injury concretely enough to come up with appropriate remedies. Apology itself could not be remedy enough, I argued. My first reservation was that there had been "a clear violation of my academic rights, and not just my personal sensibilities." I wrote that the second injury was "not to me personally, but to the students, to this faculty, and to this university," for the substitute syllabus taught to students was not only substandard but its content "a poisonous introduction for students entering a post-apartheid university" and "wrestling with the legacy of racism." I concluded that the appropriate remedy in this context was twofold: first, to lift my suspension from teaching the course, and second, "to review and radically revise" the course "under the intellectual leadership of the Professor of African Studies so as to ensure minimum conditions for the pursuit of excellence."

The faculty board immediately lifted my suspension from teaching, but did not confirm my intellectual leadership of the course as Professor of African Studies. Instead, it asked me to present in detail my objections to the course content to a meeting involving the Senior Deputy Vice Chancellor, the Dean, those who had designed the substitute syllabus and those involved with the introduction of academic programs in the university. I did this on March 23.

The group resolved to invite me on board the course team, but only as one of its members. In other words, the team would consider my critique and make changes only where they were persuaded to do so. I said I could not with intellectual integrity join and share responsibility for a course I had argued was seriously flawed intellectually and morally. The meeting felt my critique had not been discussed fully for lack of sufficient time and that it should be available in writing for full consideration. I said I would be delighted to write it, but that I would present it, not to a meeting, but to an open seminar, for review by my peers; thus taking the critique out of the administrative domain and into the academic domain.

The key question before us is: how to teach Africa in a post-apartheid academy? To answer this question, I will begin with some remarks on how Africa has been taught in the past. Historically, African Studies developed outside Africa, not within it. It was a study of Africa, but not by Africans. The context of this development was colonialism, the Cold War and apartheid. This period shaped the organization of social science studies in the Western academy. The key division was between the disciplines and area studies. The disciplines studied the white experience as a universal, human, experience; area studies studied the experience of people of color as an ethnic experience.

African Studies focused mainly on Bantu administration, customary law, Bantu languages, and anthropology. This orientation was as true of African Studies at the University of Cape Town as it was of other area study centers.

Introductory courses in African Studies usually followed a threefold division. Part One would cover Africa before the white presence, then would follow Africa under white control, and finally, there would be a section on Africa after the departure of the white man. The moral of the story, implicit or explicit, would be that things fell apart once the white man departed.

The meaning of Africa would change with the beginning of white control. Africa would cease to be the entire continent.

North Africa would become part of the Middle East, considered civilized, even if just barely. White-controlled Africa in the south would be considered an exception, an island of civilization, studied separately. Africa, popularly known as "darkest Africa," would refer geographically to equatorial Africa, and socially to black Africa, or Bantu Africa, or Negro Africa, variously so-called.

I would like to say a few words about my own work. I wrote a book in 1996 called *Citizen and Subject*. One of its objectives was to locate South Africa in the African experience. I argued that the South African academy, even when it was opposed to apartheid politically, was deeply affected by it epistemologically. "The notion of South African exceptionalism," I wrote, "is a current so strong in South African studies that it can be said to have taken on the character of a prejudice."

In my first seminar at UCT in November 1996, I said the following: "To create a truly African Studies, one would first have to take head-on the notion of South African exceptionalism and the widely shared prejudice that while South Africa is a part of Africa geographically, it is not quite culturally and politically, and certainly not economically. It is a point of view that I have found to be a hallmark of much of the South African intelligentsia, shared across divides: white or black, left or right, male or female."

My point is simple: At no point did I hide my views. I spelled them out both to the UCT Selection Committee that interviewed me in early 1996 and to over 100 members of the Faculty who came to my opening seminar in late 1996. No one should claim surprise.

Let us now come to the design of the Africa core course in the faculty's foundation semester. Let us look at the lecture outline, so I may make a few observations.

One, the course is divided in three parts, titled pre-colonial, colonial and post-colonial. But the headings are misleading. Part two actually does not begin with colonialism but with the European slave trade. The study of colonialism really begins with lecture 15 in week eight. The pre-colonial section is actually half the lectures in the course. The point is that the periodization is highly racialized. Part One is Africa before the white presence; Part Two is Africa under white control, and Part Three is Africa after the white man relinquished political control.

A second observation. Once slavery begins in equatorial Africa and the white presence in South Africa, South Africa ceases to be part of the course. In fact, both North and South Africa move out of the picture. The focus of the course narrows to equatorial Africa.

The relevant question at this point is: Could this course have been designed differently? Are there other ways of teaching the African experience that could have formed the starting point for the Africa core of UCT's Foundation Semester? My answer is: Yes.

The starting points of a different curriculum, a deracialized curriculum, were forged in the academy in independent Africa. In the course design that I prepared before I was suspended from the course in early December 1997, and in the paper I have circulated for this seminar, I suggested four crucial debates that could provide the starting point of framing a new deracialized curriculum. An awareness of the debates would have transformed each of the three parts of the substitute course that was put in place after I was suspended.

Debate One: Is a Historical Sociology of Africa Possible?

The first debate was sparked off by the work of the Senegalese scholar, Cheikh Anta Diop. Diop was concerned about how to arrive at a knowledge of Africa before the white presence. Part of the then prevailing wisdom was that, since Africa had few written languages, there were few reliable sources of knowledge —mainly archaeology, maybe oral history—for the study of Africa.

Diop's problem was one of sources of knowledge. Was it possible to go beyond archaeological sources that illuminate the distant past, from a million years ago, and oral history, which cannot go any farther than a hundred years, and link these two through other forms of knowledge? How do you reconstruct the middle ground to give historical depth to the African experience?

Diop looked for written sources in languages other than those European, mainly Arabic sources before the Moroccan invasion of Timbuktu in the 15th century. He also explored linguistic evidence. On this basis, he wrote an outline historical sociology of West Africa for the millennium between ancient Egypt and the beginning of the Atlantic Slave Trade.

Debate Two: Historicizing Gender

I want to link Diop to one of his sympathetic critics, Ifi Amadiume. Ifi's work focuses on the history of gender relations. Starting with a distinction between biological sex and social gender, she argues that the history of gender in Africa is not the same as that in Europe. In the process, she raises the larger question of the historicity of the African experience. In doing so, she moves away both from Eurocentric and from nationalist and negritude historians. Ironically, both Eurocentrists and nationalists were content simply to point out that Africa too had cities, an urban life, specialized crafts, and international trade. Her preoccupation, as that of Diop, and the generation of historians like Wamba-dia-Wamba, Mamadou Diouf, and Mohamed Mbodj, whether they agreed with Diop or not, was to illuminate the specific trajectory, or trajectories, of the African experience. Like Diop, Amadiume too is concerned to go beyond archaeology and anthropology and construct a historical sociology of Africa.

If taken into account, these two debates would have transformed the content of parts one and three of the substitute course. It would have made the first part truly interdisciplinary, instead of being confined to archaeology. It would have undercut the essentialist notions of an unchanging African economy and society that are central to the leadings in part three.

While these two debates problematize the long *duree* of African history, the relevance of debates three and four lies in that they problematize the colonial experience.

Debate Three: Reconstructing Africa from a Political Economy and Civilizational Perspective

It is well known that higher education in equatorial Africa has been mainly a post-independence achievement. As the new intelligentsia in the post-colonial academy reached out to one another, they formed a continental network, called CODESRIA (Council for the Development of Social Research in Africa). This network provided a forum for debate, a springboard of ideas that could provide a starting point for reshaping Africa as an object of study, this time decolonized and deracialized. A key intellectual contribution to this project came from Samir Amin. In the article I circulated for this seminar, I point to two key readings of Samir Amin, which I think illuminate the relevance of his contribution for an introductory course on Africa.

The first reading that I thought important was his 1972 article in the *Journal of Modern African Studies*. In this article, Samir Amin proposes a way of thinking of Africa, particularly its equatorial and southern parts, as a differentiated unity. The article is written from the standpoint of political economy and it looks at Africa as a contradictory unity of modes of productions, demarcating, for example, labor reserves from peasant economies.

The second reading is the first chapter of his 1976 book, *Unequal Development*. This time, the standpoint is that of civilizational processes, not political economy. The chapter is concerned with the impact of the Atlantic slave trade on the civilizational trajectory of Africa. What, he asks, was the civilizational consequence of the fact that the Atlantic slave trade undercut the trans-Saharan trade and the Indian Ocean trade? How crucial was this development in the production of Africa as not only sub-Saharan but also continental (adrift from the Indian Ocean islands)? In historicizing it, he problematizes the notion of sub-Saharan Africa: Africa is not a given, we make it as we make our own history.

While Samir Amin tried to build a differentiated notion of Africa from a political economy and civilizational perspective, the fourth debate I have in mind pursued this same project from a political standpoint.

Debate Four: Reconstructing Africa from a Political Standpoint

The Dar-es-Salaam debate that followed the publication of Issa Shivji's writings in the 1970s focused particularly on the nature of the state and political processes. One outcome of that debate, in the 1990s, has been to locate apartheid within the African colonial experience. The argument is as follows: Did not apartheid, as a form of the state, seek to reproduce race as an identity that would unite its beneficiaries and ethnicity as an identity that would unite its victims? To that extent, should apartheid not be understood as the generic form of the colonial state in Africa, rather than being an exception to it? Also, should we not understand the political identities that colonialism tried to institutionalize as neither positivist (that they exist), nor ideological (that they are invented) but historicized as institutionally reproduced?

My argument is that UCT's introductory course on Africa should have been structured around these four debates. If that had been the case, the first two would have problematized the long *duree* and the last two the colonial experience. If you look at the reading list of the substitute course actually taught in the Faculty, you will find none of the key African intellectuals in it.

The required readings in the substitute, instead, come from a single course text, called *Africa*, and edited by Martin Phyllis and Patrick O'Meara. Originally written in 1976, it was revised twice, first in the 1980s, and then in the 1990s. Its structure was, however, cast in 1976: that Africa is equatorial and Bantu. Subsequent revisions were informed by debates in the American academy: leading to an emphasis on political economy in the 1980s, and urbanization and gender in the 1990s. Needless to say, the revisions left its core orientation unchanged.

In my view, it was a mistake to look for a single text for the course. For the simple reason that African Studies is radically in need of revision, no single satisfactory text exists as yet.

Why then did the course team adopt a single text? Most likely, because it was the easiest thing to do, given that they had little time on hand. For those of you who have read Martin Hall's response to my paper, you will recall that Hall was approached to become a part of the course team in early December 1997, exactly when I was suspended from the course. He says he didn't begin work until mid-January. So, instead of putting together a collection of articles from diverse sources, something that would have required both expertise and time, they looked for a single text; in my view, that was an easy, lazy and irresponsible option.

Part 2: A Response to Martin Hall

Martin Hall has circulated a response to my critique. I would like to present a point-by-point consideration of his views.

First, allow me to redirect your attention to my key question: why did the focus of the substitute course narrow to equatorial Africa with the beginning of the slave trade?

Martin Hall doesn't answer this question. He does not answer it because the narrowing takes place with parts two and three, which he tells us were not his responsibility. He tells us he had nothing to do with designing them, and yet he claims, all along, that the course was team-designed!

Instead, he defends his own turf, the first part of the course. So he presents a defense of archaeology and misses the point of my central criticism. For my criticism was never that archaeology is unimportant. I had raised Diop's central question: can we go beyond archaeology and oral history and find other sources of knowledge in our understanding of Africa's history? Is it possible to construct a historical sociology for Africa, as is constructed for other parts of the world?

I still think that the exclusion of a historical sociology from part one was something forced on Martin Hall. The absence reflects a key weakness of the Department of History at UCT. That department has made choices over the past decade, so that it has no one with a research focus on equatorial Africa. This is in sharp contrast to UWC, whose Department of History invested resources precisely in that field. This is why I called on my colleagues to set aside their narrow cliquish camaraderie, their patronizing and matronizing attitudes, and tap the rich, intellectual resources at UWC.

This is why, when I was asked to design the course in early October of last year, I turned for assistance to Dr. Ibrahim Abdullah, a historian at UWC. I said in my paper that he prepared bibliographical suggestions for me, and guided my reading on the historical sections. I should have acknowledged more: for the fact is that he was the person with whom I bounced ideas every time I wrote, or rewrote, the draft of a section of the syllabus.

The second point in Hall's response relates to my second question: Why did the course team ignore all the key debates in the post-colonial African academy? Hall has three different answers to this question, each equally unsatisfactory.

He begins by saying that the reverse was the case, that he actually taught students the importance of debate and evidence. This, of course, is not the point. My question is about particular debates—those debates in the African academy that established the possibility of decolonizing and deracializing the study of Africa.

I was initially thrown by Hall's second attempt to answer this question. He brings out a long list of African names he says are referenced in the text the students read. It is like someone producing a long list of names in an intellectual debate on Freud, Marx, Einstein, etc. and protesting that some of his best friends are Jews! One would dismiss this as a trivial and patronizing gesture if it were not also revealing. For Hall shows a half-baked familiarity with these sources. I will cite the most damning instance. The list of African authors he says students read about included Ki-Zerbo and Olderogge, who he writes are from Rwanda. Now, Joseph Ki-Zerbo is from Burkina Faso, not Rwanda, something most historians around this continent would know since Ki-Zerbo was the Editor of Volume One of UNESCO's *History of Africa*. And Olderogge, I believe, is not even an African. He is a Russian, a member of the Russian academy who wrote the first Russian study of the West African jihad. A little learning, as the English say, is a dangerous thing.

I found Martin Hall's third attempt to answer this question actually the most revealing. Students, he says, "were not assigned primary sources for the first five weeks," and wonders "at which point in the curriculum students should be required to make use of primary sources." When I read this, I was appalled at Hall's notion of a primary source. A primary source is a source closest to an action. In the language of an anthropologist, a primary source is a native informant. The distinction between a primary source and an intellectual is that a primary source reports, narrates, is the source of empirical data in the first instance, whereas an intellectual sifts through this, analyzes, synthesizes, and theorizes. Now, what makes Martin Hall an intellectual, and Cheikh Anta Diop a "primary source," or a native informant? The idea that natives can only be informants, and not intellectuals, is part of an old imperial tradition. It is part of the imperial conviction that natives cannot think for themselves; they need tutelage. That this notion should have found fertile ground in apartheid South Africa with its project of Bantu education cannot be surprising. But why should it flourish unchecked in a post-apartheid academy whose ambition it is to be a world-class African university?

We need to put this in context. For the same Martin Hall who writes of natives as informants in one place lavishes praise on Diop at another. Clearly, Hall cannot help acknowledging Diop as a towering intellectual in his conscious moments. But these moments are punctuated by lapses, each a sort of a twitch, returning him to the prejudice that natives can be no more than informants. I suggest we leave further analysis of this to psychologists.

Hall says students read of Diop in his book, and he cites the relevant section in footnote 6 of his paper. Listen to what students read of Diop in Martin Hall's book. They read of "the work of Negritude historians such as Diop (who)... has emphasised the importance of Egypt's past in understanding the full sweep of Africa's history, and of Africa's contribution to the history of the Mediterranean and Europe." I have two observations on this. Since when did Diop become "a Negritude historian"? It is also clear that Hall has accessed Diop through the North American academy, and not through post-independence African debates. As I observed in my paper, "While the debate around Diop in the North American academy has revolved around his claim that ancient Egypt is the core civilizational archive of African history, Diop's larger significance lay in the more general question he raised: whether history before the arrival of the white man could be understood as a social history for historical sociology, or whether the limits of our understanding were the limits of archaeology, however unreconstructed." Hall, having missed Diop's larger significance, passes on that lack to his students.

We come to Hall's third line of defense. He has a long section statistically describing the students taking this course, underlining the fact that they are mainly from disadvantaged backgrounds. My question is: so what?

If this is meant as a justification of imparting skills through a foundation semester, that is not under discussion here. But Martin Hall's long digression does raise a question that I am sure Hall never intended: Why is this disadvantaged student body being fed a disadvantaged curriculum? Is UCT in the process of creating its own version of Bantu education?

Hall's final defense is to turn to student evaluations. He gives us the results of a student poll. Students loved the course, he says. And students, I suppose the implication is, could not possibly be wrong. My view is different. I think Martin Hall has given us a self-serving interpretation of the poll.

I have argued that the problem with this course is the result mainly of what the course team left out of the course, not of what they included in it. My critique is mainly about what they did not teach, not about what they did teach.

Students only know what they were taught; they do not know what they were not taught. If a course confirms student prejudices, prejudices instilled through Bantu education—that Africa lies north of the Limpopo, and that this Africa has no intelligentsia with writings worth reading—and if the students say they love the course, do we have anything more than successful Bantu education, now taught to black and white students in the same classroom, rather than in segregated facilities?

Student appraisals cannot substitute for a peer review process. Only demagogues would trade in one for the other, trying to silence critics by waving student appraisals in their faces. Who does not know that every enlightened dictator habitually organizes popular referenda while silencing critics through perks or punishment?

The Role of Expertise in a University

I want to deal with the final point in Martin Hall's response, because I think it deserves consideration on its own. Hall argues that there is no room for expertise in a democracy. He posits two alternatives: either there is "professorial control" or "a democratic model of participatory course planning and teaching." And he holds up the substitute course as a model of participatory design. I have already pointed out that when it comes to taking responsibility, he takes responsibility for only the first part of the course. He says literally nothing in defense of parts two and three. Is the claim to participatory planning and teaching any more than posturing?

But I want to examine the theoretical significance of Hall's argument, the argument that opposes the recognition of expertise to a democratic process. What are we to make of this latter-day Luddite position?

Universities, I hope we all agree, are about the pursuit of excellence. This is the reason why universities like to recognize, honor, and encourage expertise. That, in my view, does not rule out democracy in an intellectual setting, for democracy combines acknowledging expertise alongside keeping it open to question, professorships along with peer review. This is why scholarship needs to go hand in hand with humility. Expertise is never final. Debate is never closed. This is why vice chancellors should resist the temptation to close debates administratively, and why—in spite of Hall's claim—intellectual leadership is not the same thing as intellectual hegemony.

So long as intellectual activity is pursued within institutional boundaries, its organization hinges on decisions which impact on the lives of others. Who is qualified to make these decisions? Who is qualified to design a course syllabus? Anyone?

Let me bring this closer to home. When the university established a Chair in African Studies and recruited an academic from outside, was that not saying the university lacked expertise in the field, I might add, for understandable historical reasons?

Is not that why you invited this same person, the holder of the A. C. Jordan Chair in African Studies, to write the syllabus of an introductory course on Africa in October 1997?

Why then, when three of your members disagreed with him, instead of calling a meeting to discuss that disagreement, you, the assistant dean, suspended the person from the course the day before he was to hand you the final syllabus?

To your credit, you recognized a mistake had been made and apologized. In the meantime, you had put in place a substitute course. When your Chair in African Studies told you the substitute introductory course on Africa was seriously flawed intellectually and morally, you turned around and accused him of wanting to establish intellectual hegemony!

He has elaborated his critique of the substitute course and its three parts. In the face of the critique, Martin Hall has defended the first part. No one has defended the second part, or the third part. And no one even admits to having designed the whole course. I would like to ask: Who designed the overall course? Anyone? Or did three people design three separate parts and just slap them together?

Is participatory democracy the name of a new game in which faceless people can make decisions and hide behind the wall of democracy to avoid accountability? Is participatory democracy turning into a slogan for defending faceless decision-making? Are we in a brave new world where democracy is the swansong for a regime of non-accountability, a non-transparent regime?

Conclusion

I am aware that sections of the press have tried to sensationalize this debate, and package it as a race issue. I am also aware that some in the university have helped them do so. I want to be honest. Race is not absent from this issue, but this is not a question that pits black against white. Broadly, it is a question about curriculum transformation, and about who should be making these decisions. Narrowly, it is a question about how Africa is to be taught in a post-apartheid academy.

Students are being taught a curriculum which presumes that Africa begins at the Limpopo, and that this Africa has no intelligentsia worth reading. This version of Bantu education, of Bantu Studies called African Studies, is already being taught to every entering student in the social sciences, and will be compulsorily taught, force-fed, to every first year social science student from here on unless we, the faculty, say no.

I say that the faculty has a right to decide what students will be taught, not just how they will be taught. This decision is normally made through appointments. By all means, appoint as professor of African Studies the person whose vision of African Studies is in accord with that of the faculty. But having done so, for all our sakes, leave that person room for intellectual creativity and intellectual leadership—whoever that professor of African Studies may be!

Notes

This bulk of this article is made up of remarks by Professor Mamdani at the Seminar on the Africa Core of the Foundation Course for the Faculty of Social Sciences and Humanities, University of Cape Town, 1998. These remarks were published in *Chimurenga*, vol. 2, July 2002, http://www.chimurenga.co.za.

The Study of International Relations in South Africa: Still More Questions than Answers

Peter Vale

I

Shortly after apartheid ended, I found myself at a get-together organized by an in-house think-tank associated with the British Foreign and Commonwealth Office. In the leafy surrounds of West Sussex, the conferees were hosted in the grandest tradition of rustic living—fine meals, good wine, country walks, and a rich exchange of political ideas—mostly on South and southern Africa's future. A member of the House of Lords, who had been prominent in Margaret Thatcher's cabinet, performed the opening; she regaled the gathered with an anecdotal account of her own role in the overthrow of minority rule in South Africa. She told us how, on the prompting of her businessman husband, she set her career goals—one of which was to end apartheid. And then, without irony, she said how happy she was that this particular goal had been achieved. When she was done, the South Africans in the room were gobsmacked: one eventually put up a hand. "Thank you for explaining this to us, Baroness," a voice in an overstated South African accent said, "I had always thought that South Africa's people had ended apartheid."

The appropriation of the victory over apartheid by the international community has many sides to it. An unanticipated one is the outsourcing of the public voice of South Africa's international relations—and the compass of its foreign policy—to non-native South Africans. The purpose of this point is not to smuggle in a mindless critique of a new policy establishment and to question either their expertise or indeed their anti-apartheid credentials—after all, patriotism, as Samuel Johnson is reported to have said, is the last refuge of the scoundrel—neither is the intention to fan the already dangerous flames of xenophobia that have delivered such damage to the new South Africa.

More appositely, perhaps, the idea of patriotism as a source of higher knowing is an obvious contradiction when presented from within an academic discipline that has been near obsessed with promoting, through the idea of globalization, the very antithesis of patriotism. And certainly events both on the historical and contemporary ground seem to prove that there is no link between place of birth and place (or passion) of public service. Che Guevara, Cuban revolutionary leader, freedom fighter and now an international icon, was born in the Argentine. And, to draw a perhaps more appropriate comparison, in 2004 an Italian-born woman had to resist the entreaties of a great patriotic party to become prime minister of the world's largest democracy, India. If anything, the experience of post-apartheid South Africa points in the same direction: perhaps the most authoritative voice in the country's public policy is an Iranian-born economist with a Ph.D. from Canada's Simon Fraser University.[1]

Within the focus of this discussion—South Africa's international relations community—these new voices have certainly bought a greater representation. Unquestionably, too, this new voice has confirmed something that the notorious Broederbond was never able to grasp: that the language of South Africa's international relations (indeed, all international relations) is English.

II

Sadly, however, policy entrepreneurs, amongst them these new voices, have reasserted a feature of the discipline that the Broederbond treasured: the discipline of International Relations in South Africa is an intellectual enterprise that displays little imagination and almost no conceptual adventure. There are important exceptions to this rule, but space does not permit their listing. This absence of daring and the accompanying lack of adventure were not always so; there was a moment when South Africa's future in the world was pregnant with possibilities and it is worth recalling what happened to it.

The euphoria that characterized the ending of the Cold War masked great uncertainty in both governments and their institutions. Why? Most importantly, perhaps, those near-Archimedean beacons of surety and security in Cold War International Relations—East and West—were suddenly without anchorage. This explains why the policy questions that were asked at the time reflected both bewilderment and befuddlement. Here follows a random selection drawn from memory. What will become of the Soviet Union? And what will happen to its nuclear weapons? Why is Yugoslavia breaking up? Should we recognize Bosnia? How do you spell Herzegovina? Is globalization a noun or a verb? Must America dominate? Where next for Marxism? Which Rwanda matters?

In contrast to this uncertainty, the issue of South Africa, despite some initial skepticism, sustained a recognizable political parabola. So, for instance, the fate of the white minority and the black majority continued to be discussed on a register that was familiar to politicians and policy makers. In addition, the conditions and conditionalities of the proposals and the eventual political settlement in the country were discussed in English, a tongue that was readily accessible to many across the world. These reasons, and many others besides, suggest why South Africa became (to use a cliché which Moletsi Mbeki uses on page 14 of the *2002/3 South African Yearbook of International Affairs*) "the flavor of the month."

That was a moment when Nelson Mandela began to look like a bridge between the past and the future—between black and white, between communist and capitalist, between injustice past and integrity future. It was an instant when the unfolding of events in South Africa became a kind of aperture through which humanity could view a common destiny. Indeed, South Africa's moral leadership of a disorientated world seemed to be perfectly scripted by the Welsh maxim, *A fo ben, bid bont*—He who would be a leader, let him be a bridge.[2]

However, as Mandela was being lauded, the specter of a reassertion of American sovereign power emerged through the trope offered by U.S. President George Herbert Walker Bush, "a new world order." The idea of ordering the world quickly filtered into the discourse around South Africa's International

Relations and helped return the disciple from the hands of the so-called "radicals" to the self-styled "realists."[3] In a famous line borrowed from the Sex Pistols, South Africa was then pronounced to be "just another country."[4] These developments helped to domesticate International Relations in South Africa into the emerging codes of a new authoritarianism that was first seen in the Gulf War, later in the Allied bombing of Iraq and the war in the Kosovo.

South Africa's international relations establishment was quick to celebrate this closing of the South African mind—to borrow the conservative American literary theorist Allan Bloom's famous phrase.[5] Arguably, however, they have gone a tad further than they or their patrons expected because, far too often for comfort, the South Africans appear to be openly complicit in the policy routines that underpin what the late Susan Sontag called "the doctrines of world struggle."[6] This may seem to be unfair, but is there another way to explain how the national director of the "country's foremost think-tank" the South African Institute of International Affairs,[7] was in a position to write reports from the frontline as British troops invaded Iraq?[8]

The purpose of recalling this recent history is to situate the voice of South Africa's International Relations within a moment in which the discourse on global affairs is increasingly caught between two conceptual purposes of the study itself—the familiar ontological space occupied by state sovereignty with its neat demarcations of Inside and Outside, to use Rob Walker's pithy metaphor.[9] While the second talks for those who are "marginalized and excluded, and who, for a range of reasons, reject the current [march towards] globalization."[10]

III

Notwithstanding essays from near fifty contributors to the seventh edition of the *Yearbook of International Affairs* that is the focus of this essay, there is little effort to explore the world of the excluded and the marginalized. This judgment may seem unkind to a number (or all) of these authors since there is no indication that, when asked to write on a designated topic, they were restricted to a set paradigm—to carefully choose the noun. Certainly, Elizabeth Sidiopolous, talks about "many faces, many voices" and a "vocal civil society" in her brief Introduction to the collection. But, she gets to these alternatives ways of viewing the political and the international, only after prior positioning the book in four—not three, as she has it—global events: the war on terror, the war on Iraq (which she calls "ancillary"), the continuing crisis in Zimbabwe, and the launch of the African Union.

By invoking the well worn "prisoner of a paradigm" trope in his opening chapter, Greg Mills holds out the hope that these essays will take the world of ideas seriously. However, the writing is quickly captured by policy prescriptions and entirely fails to probe "the entire constellation of beliefs, values, techniques, and so on [that] are shared by members" of the local IR community.[11] Unhappily, this is the point when the instrumental purpose offered by policy (and its making) gets confused with explanation—a confusion that occurs in many other places in the collection. The problem-solving theory which underpins this approach to International Relations aims to reinforce the global status quo, and Greg Mills is clear that the failure of South Africa's government to follow the so-called Coalition of the Willing into Iraq will do damage to South Africa's "national interest."[12] The path to this instrumentalist point of analytical entry is smoothed by "the end of history" idea which, when it comes to policy, emphasizes that economic delivery is all that matters.

Instead of delivering to South Africa's people, Mills argues, the foreign policy of Thabo Mbeki's South Africa is underlain with "an anti-Western sentiment, not informed by direct interests, but rather by a history of colonialisation ... by the socialist background of the ANC's leadership... by historical ambivalence and indeed outright opposition ... [toward] notably Margaret Thatcher and Ronald Reagan."[13] He suggests further, that South Africa's Middle East policy is shaped by religion and, "more importantly, by race, the latter the most visceral and difficult to curb legacy of South Africa's past."[14] These are sharp accusations, indeed, but meeting them does not readily belong together with the promise of deep-seated conceptual change that is the inherent in the idea of the paradigm, as enunciated in Thomas Kuhn's work and developed by others. This is a good example of how the wrong conceptual tool is used to voice a policy difference. Greg Mills' worry is how to position the liberal-hawk fashions of contemporary policy-making into the southern African region in the name of the much-vaunted idea of "regime change" especially in Zimbabwe. Paradigms, as Kuhn suggested, are not concerned with the limited choices offered by problem-solving theory; they are concerned with the fundamental assumptions of whole areas of scientific inquiry.

This same absence of reflexivity and self-reflection—often, plain contradiction—regretfully, characterizes many of the essays in this collection.

IV

In International Relations there is penchant for the review-type collection. In Canada, for example, an annual collection focuses on that country's foreign policy. Canadian David Malone, the director of the International Peace Academy, in a discussion of the latest—the nineteenth in this series—writes that it "has become a valuable teaching and research tool for those ... toiling in academic vineyards ... [and] it has been of sufficiently high quality (consistently so) that I and many others look forward to it."[15] And for many years, the Australian Institute of International Affairs have produced an annual publication which appears under the sub-title "Australia in World Affairs"—like the Canadian one, organized around a particular theme; so, for instance, the 2002 Australian publication turned on the theme, "the national interest in a global era."[16]

This thematic approach however has no place in the 2002–03 *South African Yearbook of International Affairs*. Predictably, then, the collection displays a lack of focus, notwithstanding efforts to organize the contents under five topics with a sixth, a really informative reference section, including a helpful glossary. Literarily speaking, some essays appear disjoined and, technically speaking, others are distinctly disconnected from what is probably the real overarching focus, the idea of South Africa.

Take, for example, a contribution by the well South African journalist Peter Fabricius. This is a lively and well-written piece, called "Norway the Peacemaker," but it is entirely devoid of any connection to that country's relationship with South Africa—neither the long links between the Norwegian churches and South Africa, nor the fact that one of the most important chapters in South African literature was written in Norway,[17] nor is there any exploration of Oslo's role in South Africa's own liberation.[18] Even if measured on its own terms—Norway as peacemaker—it is ahistorical and offers no theoretical reflection. The importance of the latter, of course, is in the fact—recognized, but not explored by Fabricius—that non-government actors in Norway have bolstered that country's capacity to punch way above its proverbial weight in global affairs, to use a metaphor first employed by a one-time British Foreign Secretary, Douglas Hurd.[19]

"The State of the World One Year after 11 September" is a thoughtful essay embedded in rational choice theory—the controlling and process-driven end of International Relations scholarship, as we have already noted, that is much admired in South Africa. This account sets out the issues around the Weapons of Mass Destruction (WMD) that are still to be found in Iraq. However, the impact that this contribution might well have made on the local policy community is entirely undone by a stunning lack of knowledge on the part of those who were responsible for issuing the *Yearbook*. Slocombe is not simply "with the Norwegian Nobel Institute," as the biographical note on page 381 suggests; he may well have been at the time this essay was written, but he has a longer, more impressive pedigree which well equips him to pronounce on the place of the US in the world after 9/11. A lawyer by training, Walt Slocombe has spent a lifetime of service in strategic and security studies with spells, as is the American wont, in and out of government, including a posting as Under Secretary for Defense for Policy during the Clinton Administration. Ironically, at about the time this edition of the *Yearbook* appeared, he was helping to create the new Iraq army.

Readers may think that I have been a little finicky at this point: certainly so, and with good reason. How are South Africans to understand the world without knowing who it is who is saying what, and why? After all, "Theory is always *for* someone and *for* something," as Robert Cox pointed out more than twenty years ago.[20]

V

In South Africa, the annual review that has withstood the test of time (to quote a well-known beer advertisement) is the *South Africa Survey* that is put out by the country's original think-tank, the seventy-five year old South African Institute of Race Relations (SAIRR). This particular publication started in 1933 as a two-monthly publication and changed, over the years, to a quarterly and finally, in 1946, annual production—its first name was *Race Relations*, then *Survey of Race Relations* and finally, when race relations were supposedly no longer an issue in the country, the *South Africa Survey*.[21] The publication has been associated with illustrious researchers in the tradition of South African liberalism—Ellen Hellman, Alfred Hoernlé, Leo Marquard and Edgar Brookes, to name a few.[22] For years it was edited by one of the great and unsung researchers on South Africa, Muriel Horrell. Elizabeth Sidiropolous also, interestingly, once edited it. In the country's dark days, the importance of the *Race Relations Survey* was that "after the Government Gazette, it was probably the publication most often consulted as a basic source of information about our country."[23]

The *Survey* (and through it, the SAIRR) sought to offer up information about the situation in South Africa. As the formidable Ellen Hellman once put, the SAIRR "believed in the pursuit of truth as a value in itself."[24] It was only when the intense theoretical discussion started on what constituted that kernel of all writing in the humanities, the "Social Fact," that the work of the SAIRR, and their annual survey, was questioned. These were deepened by the influence of Marxist scholarship in South Africa, although now questioned, that undoubtedly strengthened the humanities. Charles van Onselen has recently suggested that this work, especially in history, led the way "for what was to become by far, the most exciting two decades in the social sciences" in South Africa.[25] It was, incidentally, the vital question of who defines "the facts" which famously led one wag to declare that the motto of the Institute of Race Relations should have been "Forward to Freedom with Facts and Figures!"

The *South African Yearbook of International Affairs* looks as if it was modeled on *The Survey* and, like the same publication, *The Yearbook* seems not much interested in exploring the distinction between "facts" and "values." So, the truth that is presented in the book is value-laden—it has described the world and South Africa's place in it, not how the world *is* but, in the opinion of these contributors, how the world *ought* to be. In not genuflecting towards this possibility, the SAIIA, who published the *Yearbook*, have again proven the force of the old saw: "there is no more vicious a theoretician than the practical man who says, 'let the facts speak for themselves.'" Like much writing in International Relations in South Africa, this collection departs from serious South African scholarship in the humanities but, as it does so, ironically continues a well-worn national tradition in the study of International Relations—the absence of serious reflection.[26]

VI

In this particular account of its work, the SAIIA show a far too close an association with sponsorship, especially when it comes to (shall we say) the corporatization of foreign policy. This is well illustrated in Tim Hughes' celebratory account of the Kimberley Process that suggests how intimately the door between diplomacy and commerce can swing—a process, of course, assisted by institutions like this book and its publishers.[27] The same closeness is to be found in two further essays: Moletsi Mbeki's, which has already crossed our path, pleads for a "more productive foreign policy,"[28] and Greg Mills and Lyal White's "Cutting Your Coat ... Towards an Appropriate Foreign Representative Structure for SA." The latter stresses the importance to foreign policy of trade and suggests, as have the Canadians and Australians, that collapsing the bureaucratic arrangements around diplomacy into the institutions for the conduct of trade relations in South Africa will deliver the country more effective international relations.

The ideas of productivity, delivery, and problem solving imbue the spirit of modernization that bristles throughout this collection. But this is a social form in which surveillance and new forms of control are preferred to liberation, liberty, and people. And while the notion of "democracy" appears again and again in these pages, when it does it is always couched in weasel words—like "governance," "accountability," and "transparency"—which hobble its emancipatory potential.

Most of the arguments in the collection are not concerned about making a *different* world, notwithstanding the constant lip service to making a *difference in* the world. This explains why, unlike the annual Australian and Canadian collections to which we referred earlier South Africa's version appears to bypass even the ritualized social form offered by diplomacy and its study. Interestingly, eleven contributions in the heart of the enterprise, grouped under the title "Essays on Select African Themes," do try to break away from the book's ritualized formula. Of particular note is the essay on civil society, democracy, and mobilization, written by Adam Habib and Paul Opoku Mensah, which almost delivers on Elizabeth Sidiopolous' early promise of engaging civil society.

In contrast to these, almost all of the short reports in the section called "Issues in South African Foreign Policy" follow a path, not to diplomatic studies, but towards managed outcomes. Unhappily, however, they bring South African International Relations no closer to understanding some of the important questions that are asked by contemporary foreign policy analysis. What is the role of agency in the making of South Africa's foreign policy? Does President Thabo Mbeki enjoy the most important role in the making of South Africa's foreign policy? How deep is the initiating role of the bureaucracy in the making of South Africa's foreign policy? As a result, a decade after the end of apartheid, it seems that South African International Relations is no closer to understanding how the country's foreign policy is made than it was twenty years ago when Deon Geldenhuys' book, *The Diplomacy of Isolation* appeared.[29]

Indeed, any understanding of the history of writing on South Africa's foreign policy may have resolved the second question, who makes South African foreign policy? In almost the first book written on the topic nearly forty years ago, the American polymath, Ned Munger famously wrote:

> If one were to list the most important people making foreign policy (in South Africa), the names might well run: 1. Dr. Verwoerd. 2. Dr. Verwoerd. 3. Dr. Verwoerd. 4. Foreign Minister Muller. 5. The Cabinet and 6. Secretary G. P. Jooste, Brand Fourie, Donald Sole, and one or two other professionals.[30]

Zimbabwe has certainly presented post-apartheid South Africa with a conundrum that has been—near-obsessively, I must add —interrogated by the South African Institute of International Affairs. In this book, two contrasting essays—one by a citizen of that country, Martin Rupiya, and the other by the business intellectual and businessman (they are not necessarily the same), Kuseni Dlamini—stand in sharp contrast to each other. The former offers what he calls "A Zimbabwean Perspective" and briefly (but neatly) grapples with some of the historical and economic connections between the two societies. Although embedded in the coded language of sovereign interest analysis, Rupiya offers a credible account of the recent deterioration in the relations between Pretoria and Harare. But it would perhaps have been more interesting if he had used the complementary lens offered by historical sociology to provide deeper insights into issues around state formation and its twin, sovereignty.

Dlamini's version of Mbeki's policy is both ahistorical and asociological: as a result, it is riddled with the kind of cliché that offers neither real understanding nor policy prescription. It tries to cross a number of conceptual divides, but somehow avoids discussing class.

There is certainly a need for a strong, forthright but nuanced policy towards Mugabe's Zimbabwe: no one in this book and, alas, no one since, has pointed the way towards this. As a result the shibboleths round quick fixes offered by the liberal-hawks persist notwithstanding the failure in Iraq.

VII

Notwithstanding the exaggerated claim of the British baroness, South Africa's people did free themselves. The international domestication of the country's International Relations and the insistence that foreign policy should be managed and controlled has certainly stilled the high ideals that South Africa held out to a befuddled world a short decade ago. Where are these now? What is their currency? Nowhere and nothing, seems to be the answer, especially if this collection, like its predecessors, is taken to be "the indispensable guide to South Africa's foreign policy"—as the book jacket reports *The Star* in Johannesburg as saying.

Yet because South Africa's people were victorious, every reader of these 450 pages must recognize that the country has a vital interest—to deliberately choose a loaded term from the controlled sub-discipline of Strategic Studies—in a range of international issues that are not addressed between these covers. Listing them as questions, as I will presently do, not only points to the far too many silences in this collection, but also will serve to remind South Africa's International Relations that the discipline's civic engagement did not begin with the new arrivals. Many academic disciplines—especially International Relations—were implicated in the destructive language of power and the codes of authoritarianism that marked apartheid's rise and fall. That was a time when the promise of modernity, like now, was yoked to a meta-theoretical idea. Then it was called the

Cold War and Separate Development; today, it takes many forms: Globalization, War on Terror, Democratic Regimes; the list is endless. In its earlier form, this forces routine of power and authority—dressed up as a form of knowing—allowed battalions of crackpots to wash up on these shores in order to teach (and to preach) the very canon of *realpolitik* that has returned to scar the public face of International Relations in South Africa.

So, as this book speaks of Terror, why is there no mention of South Africa's own ruinous experience with this idea? As this book speaks of Human Rights, why is there no mention of the 595 prisoners held in Guantánamo Bay, where the idea of sovereignty has surely reached a new level of farce? As this book speaks of Africa's place in the world why are the seven words – "sought significant quantities of uranium [from Africa]" - spoken by the forty-third president of the United States, as he justified the euphemism called "Shock and Awe," not subjected to searching critique? As this book speaks of southern Africa's future, why is there an eerie silence over whether Lesotho and Swaziland have a place in a greater South Africa?[31] As this book speaks of race, why have these pages not turned to Franz Fanon for understanding, if not for answers? As this book speaks of Sudan, why were the expert opinions to be found in these pages not able to predict the holocaust that has recently occurred in Darfur? As this book obsesses about Robert Mugabe (whose face glares out from the front cover), why is there no thick description of political events in that country? As this book thinks aloud about the idea of security, why is there no dedicated discussion of southern Africa's only real security worry, water?

Ten years have shown that post-apartheid South Africa matters to the world; because this is so, as we have often been reminded, the country, too punches above its weight in international affairs. This is why the pathology of International Relations in South Africa should be a matter of serious enquiry. Ideas make the world and annual reviews, like the *South African Yearbook of International Affairs*, are forums for the promotion of these; this is why this collection (and the format it takes) matters both at home and abroad. Yet it punches way, way below its weight because South Africa's voice in international relations has been domesticated: the reasons for this are plain to see in a book with no intellectual compass, lacking in conceptual adventure and whose contributors are far more anxious about potentates than they are offended by the conditions faced by those at the margins of economic globalization which this book celebrates.

Until this changes, alas, writing about the writing of International Relations in South Africa, because it feeds off the negative,[32] will remain a dismal duty in a doomed but still very dangerous discipline.

Notes

1. *Mail and Guardian* (Johannesburg), April 30, 2004, p.19.
2. The idea for this comes from *The Penguin Dictionary of International Relations,* edited by Graham Evans and Jeffrey Newnham. Graham Evans, who had written much on South Africa's foreign policy, died in 2003. In fondly remembering him, I want to pay tribute to a generous and funny man with many, many gifts and wonderful ideas.
3. *Mail and Guardian* (Johannesburg), September 8, 1995.
4. This idea came from Jack Spence, "On Becoming Just another Country," *The World Today* (1997) 53(3). For a deeper discussion of the effect this has had on South Africa's foreign policy, see Peter Vale and Ian Taylor, " South Africa's Post-Apartheid Foreign Policy Five Years On: From Pariah State to 'Just Another Country'?," *The Round Table* 352 (1999), pp. 629-34.
5. Allan Bloom, *The Closing of the American Mind* (New York: Simon and Schuster, 1987).
6. Susan Sontag, "What have we done," *The Guardian* (London), May 25, 2004.
7. John Fraser, "No Quick Fix for Africa's Troubles," *Business Day,* June 20, 2003.
8. Greg Mills, "Coalition Forces in Iraq," *Business Day* (Johannesburg), February 5, 2003.
9. Rob Walker, *Inside/Outside: International Relations as Political Theory* (Cambridge: Cambridge University Press, 1993).
10. Richard Falk, "Review of 'The Political Economy of a Plural World: Critical Reflections on Power, Morals and Civilisation' (by Robert Cox)," *Perspectives on Politics,* 2(1) (2004).
11. Thomas S. Kuhn, Thomas S. *The Structure of Scientific Revolutions* (Chicago: University of Chicago Press, 1962), p. 175.
12. South African Institute of International Affairs, *South African Yearbook of International Affairs: 2002-2003* (Braamfontein: South African Institute of International Affairs, 2003), p. 6.

13. *Ibid.*, p.3.
14. *Ibid.*, p.3, n.11.
15. David M. Malone, "A Question of Style," *Literary Review of Canada* 12:2 (2004), p. 3
16. James Cotton and John Ravenhill, ed., *The National Interest in a Global Era: Australia in World Affairs 1996-2000* (Sydney: Oxford University Press, 2002).
17. The opening lines of Alan Paton's *Cry, the Beloved Country* were written in the Hotel Bristol in Trondheim, Norway, on September 24, 1946.
18. An account of this can be found in Tore Linne Eriksen, *Norway and National Liberation in Southern Africa* (Uppsala: Nordiska Afrikainstitutet, 2002).
19. A brief discussion of both South Africa and Norway as so-called Middle Powers is to be found in Peter Vale, "Out of the World of Shadow Boxing," *Leadership* 13:5 (1994), pp. 58-61.
20. Robert Cox, "Social Forces and World Orders: Beyond International Relations Theory," *Millennium. Journal of International Relations* 10: 2 (1981), p. 128.
21. This information was generously emailed to me by Jane Tempest of the South African Institute of Race Relations on May 19, 2004.
22. Perhaps South Africa's first real political scientist, Edgar Brookes had a distinguished career in the South African Institute of Race Relations and in the country's Senate where he represented Africans. He wrote an early book on South Africa's International Relations, *South Africa in a Changing World* (Cape Town: Oxford University Press, 1953).
23. "After the *Government Gazette*, it was clearly the most widely consulted publication for basic information about our land." Peter Vale, "Om Rasseverhoudinge te Bevorder," *Die Suid-Afrikaan* 3 (1985), p. 29.
24. Vale, "Om Rasseverhouding te Bevorder," p. 29.
25. Charles Van Onselen, *Address delivered on receiving an Honorary Doctorate from Rhodes University*, April 2, 2004 (mimeo), p. 5.
26. See Peter Vale, "'Whose World is it Anyway': International Relations in South Africa," in Hugh C Dyer and Leon Mangasarian, ed., *The Study of International Relations: The State of the Art* (London: Macmillan, 1989), p. 207.
27. This phrase is borrowed from "Muddying the rules on asylum," *The Economist*, January 13, 1996, p.17.
28. SAIIA, *South African Yearbook*, pp.13-19, n.11.

29. Deon Geldenhuys, *The Diplomacy of Isolation: South African Foreign Policy Making* (Johannesburg: Macmillan, 1984).
30. Edwin S. Munger, *Notes on the Formation of South African Foreign Policy* (Pasadena, California: The Castle Press, 1965), p. 85.
31. F. K. Makoa, "Debates about Lesotho's Incorporation into the Republic of South Africa: Ideology versus National Survival," *Africa Insight*, 26: 4 (1996), pp. 347-53.
32. This is a phrase was introduced to me by my colleague, the political philosopher Dr. Tony Fluxman.

Gender and Women's Studies in Post-Apartheid South Africa

Sheena Essof

Introduction

Gender and women's studies is viewed as an innovative transdisciplinary field, deriving its impetus from the work of feminist academics. In African academic institutions it responds to the particular challenges facing African women intellectuals and activists and the experiences of African women's movements. The institutional spread of this field is discussed in this article, as are the changing strategic directions of two key sites, with a view to highlighting the challenges and the potential of feminist intellectual work. Throughout feminist intellectual work is conceptualized as offering valuable methodological and analytical approaches that facilitate the development of critical intellectual capacities. These are defined as being capacities that draw on cutting-edge critical theory, that are critical of the global status quo, and that are critical to ensuring that Africans can proactively address the myriad challenges facing the development and transformation of the region in the twenty-first century.

In African contexts, the intensification of contradictions between policy and practice, between the rhetoric of rights and the reality of neoliberal economic strategies informs and energizes many kinds of counter-hegemonic intellectual activity.

143

The persistence of gender injustice and inequality in all major postcolonial political and social institutions, including Africa's under resourced and beleaguered campuses, also stimulates critical reflection among the growing pool of educated women in Africa in and beyond the academy. There has been a deepening interest in feminist-inspired intellectual work, and this is reflected in the remarkable proliferation of sites engaging in gender and women's studies in many parts of Africa during the recent decades. However, the contradictory conditions under which this interest has grown also present their own challenges and constraints.

The following analysis identifies four conditions that can be seen to have fuelled the development of gender and women's studies in African contexts. The first of these is the broader development of political consciousness inspired by women's political engagement both during colonial rule and since independence. This has led to a greater awareness and acceptance of the emancipation of women as an integral and necessary facet of African liberation and development in general.

Secondly, the internationalization of feminism, and the resulting manifestation of gender discourses within international agencies and national governments—however tempered—can be seen to have stimulated intellectual, activist, and policy interests in involving women in modernization, and this has been reflected in development policies. That this has tended to reflect integrationist and instrumentalist approaches to "the woman question" is self-evident with the benefit of hindsight.

Third, gender studies has benefited from the gradual but steady growth in the overall numbers of women gaining access to higher education, and their related exposure to diverse intellectual resources and influences.

Fourth, the political, historical and economic conditions of African intellectual development have inevitably generated much critical engagement with Western intellectual legacies, notably those around the exclusionary legacies of Western ivory tower universities, the disciplinary organization of knowledge, and the methodologies for the production of knowledge. These have never seemed to make intellectual, organizational or financial sense to scholars confronted with the enormous challenges facing underdeveloped societies, and the demand for a socially responsive and responsible intelligentsia. These popular pressures have given rise to interest in socially engaged and transdisciplinary intellectual directions on several fronts—one of which is gender studies.[1]

Feminism and Development

Feminism is taken here to refer quite simply to the political and intellectual movement for the liberation of women. As it has arisen in diverse contexts, feminism can be traced to many disparate trajectories, some reflecting highly localized responses to particular conditions, while others are decidedly transnational in their reach and importance.

In African contexts, it is now well established that women were actively involved in the early-mid-twentieth century anticolonial and nationalist struggles that led up to independence and the establishment of modern nation-states. The ensuing period has seen women's activism continuing, but now being directed at the state structures that women helped to craft. The attainment of nation-statehood has made it incumbent on women to pursue their integration into public life, and much energy has been devoted to lobbying for legal and policy reforms and demanding women's equal representation in the hierarchies of power and fairer access to resources. The political premise of this state-focused mode of activism reflects great faith in all the political and public sector institutions that women, like men, had fought and worked to establish, and in which they later often found employment. In other words, women, as devotees and citizens of the new nations, deserved a fair share of public resources and access to opportunities, as well as to modern legal rights and protections.

As a result of both local and international activism, women have indeed achieved significant political, legal, and policy reforms, and governments have been pushed to set up national structures responsible for "women's affairs." The efficacy of these legal and policy reforms and government structures ostensibly instituted to address the articulated interests of women has varied, but by and large been limited in ways that continue to provoke critical debate.[2] Their efficacy has been further compromised in the context of the retraction of the public sector within which all such gains are located. The fact is that neoliberal economic doctrines are depleting the provision of public services and support systems in ways that are having highly deleterious effects on the lives of ordinary citizens across

Africa—a growing majority of whom are already living below the poverty line. That these negative effects are compounded by the dynamics of gender inequality hardly bears repeating.

Now that the state has been rolled back (or, in some instances, has collapsed entirely), feminist analysts who once focused on the challenges posed by the bureaucratization of feminism within government and UN institutions are directing their attention at the devastating impact of globalization.[3] The poorly defined and even more poorly understood logic of "market forces" appears to be steadily supplanting even the limited benevolence and protection of states which despite decades of feminism and gender activism have by and large failed to transcend their own patriarchal premises.

In other words, feminism has made complicated inroads in the world of global development, and the gains and setbacks are the product of complex negotiations within and across the hierarchies of power that constitute and drive the development industry. Each apparent advance has generated its own challenges and risks; each maneuver has been greeted with new maneuvers. As we enter the "knowledge society," a key concern must be the global inequalities played out in the arena of knowledge production, in which I include feminist knowledge production. If the interaction between feminist movements and development has generated the gender industry, then feminist interventions in African intellectual life can be said to have generated gender and women's studies, in the manner explored below.

Intellectual Development in Africa

As has been widely observed, most new nations began with a flag, an army, a civil service, and the proud establishment of at least one national university. Gross enrollment rates in African universities increased dramatically during the 1970s, from an estimated 181,000 in 1975 to over 600,000 in 1980. After a plateau in the 1980s, the figures more than doubled to over 1.75 million in 1995, and are still growing fast in most places. Despite this substantial growth, the African region still has the lowest tertiary enrollment rates in the world, with a gross enrollment rate of only 5 percent.[4] This has not prevented the sector from being targeted for financial reforms likely to constrain growth and public access and to subject institutional development to elusive market forces, likely to compromise social justice and equity agendas.

Over time, as nation-states themselves became more inward looking and neocolonial, so too did the universities servicing them. Some states claiming to be revolutionary or Marxist unleashed campaigns of terror against the intelligentsia. Authoritarian and military rulers dramatically diminished intellectual freedom even while they established new institutions. At the same time, economic decline and the imposition of international economic doctrines constrained the availability of public funding, and the quality of intellectual life deteriorated, becoming increasingly constrained, competitive, and fragmented. With hindsight it is easy to see that "national" orientation of universities remained unproblematized, and insensitive to the fact that African nations are deeply marked by gender, class, ethnicity, religion, and various other dimensions of difference and inequality. In keeping with the universal assumptions of Western liberal thought, it was assumed that differential patterns of access and inclusion would simply wither away, once formally instituted social divisions of the colonial era were abolished. Thus African universities have served as key routes to social mobility, enabling steadily increasing numbers of people on the continent to gain the credentials and training towards the pursuit of professional careers first at home, and later abroad too.[5] It is therefore worth recalling that until the crisis and reform of African higher education, locally trained doctors, lawyers, teachers, scientists, social scientists, artists, and media professionals were being produced in sufficient numbers to staff government and private sector institutions established all over the continent.

The well documented deterioration of Africa's higher education sector during the 1980s and 1990s need not be detailed here.[6] Life simply became untenable for new generations of Africans who might reasonably have been expected to play keys roles in national and regional development. Significant numbers migrated overseas, only a minority was able to pursue academic careers, and those who remained found their brains drained in other ways—into various entrepreneurial and consultancy activities that soon became more essential to their survival than their professional employment as highly trained academics. The long-term consequences of the deterioration of African higher education for the development capacities of the region, especially intellectual development, are immeasurable. One of the consequences of the decline has been the diminution of both academic freedom and institutional autonomy, not just from the state, but also more invidiously from international financial institutions and other external interests.[7]

Who are the architects of the decline and ongoing redirection of African academic institutions? While the growing leverage exercised by international financial institutions and interests during the seemingly endless economic crisis is commonly invoked, it is also clear that authoritarian governments and officials have had their own reasons for embracing external directives. However, even the more democratically inclined regimes that initially placed a premium on education eventually themselves complied with economic conditionalities, leading to the rapid erosion of educational institutions, even as demand continued to grow.

Gender Politics in African Academic Organizations

Despite the modernizing and emancipatory imperatives guiding African universities, and the gradual increase of the proportion of women accessing tertiary education, the empirical profile is one in which inequality has been sustained across the first three decades of independence. In the mid-1990s the available figures suggested that only about 3 percent of Africa's professorate were women.[8] More recent calculations indicate a high level of variation, but place the number of women faculty as between 6.1 percent in Ethiopia, 12 percent in Ghana and Nigeria, and after a decade of affirmative action, 19 percent in Uganda. Only 25 percent of students on the continent were women in the mid-1990s.[9] At the present time the statistics are still incomplete, but the percentage of women enrolled as students varies widely from a low of 9 percent in Central African Republic and 15 percent in Ethiopia, to over 40 percent in Morocco, Egypt, and Senegal. Libya and Swaziland are the only countries approximating numerical parity, both showing 51 percent.[10]

These global figures only address access to study and employment, and tell us very little about the institutional cultures and conditions facing women in Africa's universities. For the time being, deeper analysis must rely on qualitative evidence and the accumulated experience and knowledge among Africa's more gender conscious academics.[11] What is clear from these disparate sources is the fact that Africa's campuses remain difficult and challenging places for women at many levels, in ways that are complicated further by the dynamics of growing poverty and by persistently inequitable ethnic, religious, sexual, and other social relations. The persistence of patriarchal and misogynistic campus cultures, growing public sensitivity to the sexual harassment and abuse, and the complex links between sexual transactions and the spread of HIV/AIDs undoubtedly fuels interest in gender and women's studies, if not in the more assertive manifestations of feminist politics.

As a field in which women are taken seriously as scholars and intellectuals, gender and women's studies offers women students and academic staff alternative routes to academic and professional development. Gender and women's studies departments also offer women possibilities of collegial and mentoring relationships less likely to be subverted by the interpersonal dynamics of gender and sexuality. Feminist methodologies tend to be learner-centered and empowering, and to privilege collegiality and collective intellectual work, as well as a plethora of innovative research methodologies sensitive to power relations and gender dynamics. At an analytical level, feminist theory and gender analysis offer tools that problematize and explore the myriad experiences of marginalization that still constitute many aspects of women's lived experience in and beyond the academy.

Other more positive developments have occurred during the period of crisis and reform. The African intellectual community has responded in many ways, but the most strategic has been the organization of independent intellectual work outside the academic establishment. The 1970s saw the emergence of several regional scholarly associations and networks that sought to facilitate transnational intellectual dialogue. Perhaps the most significant of these are the Council for the Development of Social Science Research in Africa (CODESRIA) in 1973, and the Association of African Women for Research and Development (AAWORD) in 1982. Both were autonomous Pan-African networks which reaffirmed, and later came to sustain, earlier intellectual traditions that challenged imperial legacies and committed African scholarship to new and transdisciplinary methodologies, multilingualism, egalitarian and radical research and scholarship grounded in African social realities and concerns, and the defense of academic freedom.

During the ensuing period, as the crisis in the university sector deepened, the relative importance of the NGO sector in

African intellectual life grew, especially in terms of research and publication. In the end it is these independent bodies that have ensured the presence of a vibrant and exciting intellectual culture closely attuned to the changing conditions and challenges facing Africans at all levels of their diverse and complex societies. CODESRIA and AAWORD, both set up in the 1970s, were joined by the Addis Ababa-based Organization of Social Science Research in East Africa (OSSREA) and the Southern African Political Economy Trust (SAPES) based in Harare. Later nationally-focused NGOs like the Centre for Basic Research in Kampala and the Port Harcourt-based Centre for Advanced Social Studies and the Kano-based Centre for Research and Documentation, both in Nigeria, and the Forum for Social Studies in Addis Ababa were also established as key sites for radical research.

Women have been actively involved in bringing feminist theory and gender analysis to these forums, but they have also established a plethora of women's organizations engaging in research, documentation and training from an activist orientation. These include the Tanzanian Gender Networking Program, the Women and Laws in Southern African research network, the Zimbabwe Women's Resource Centre and Network, the Women Law and Development Network, the Nairobi-based FEMNET, the ISIS-WICCE network based in Uganda, the Southern African Network of Tertiary Institutions Challenging Sexual Harassment and Gender-based Violence, and the Feminist Studies Network, both hosted by the African Gender Institute. These more independent organizations have been valuable sites for the pursuit of feminist studies and activism in various fields.

The importance of all these independent academic organizations lies in the fact that they have enabled African intellectual life to survive the deterioration of tertiary institutions, and supported academics concerned to maintain the critical and socially responsive orientations that have been so difficult to sustain within more formal academic institutions.[12] Often able to draw on well-developed international connections for support, the activities carried out through these forums reflect a deep collective commitment to maintaining and strengthening critical intellectual work in Africa. Within the women's organizations carrying out research and documentation a close and reciprocal engagement between theory, policy and practice has always been central. However, the immediacy and intensity of lobbying and advocacy work may often have led to it taking priority over more reflective modes of intellectual engagement and reflection. What has become clearer with experience is the fact that maintaining the synergy between theory and practice, between research and activism, presents challenges that require both intellectual skill and strategic competence.

Coming back to broader societal conditions, I noted that feminist activism has made it incumbent on governments, international agencies, and other policy makers to display some level of engagement with the gender implications of development strategies, policies, and projects. This has, in turn, created a demand for gender experts who can lay claim to enough technical proficiency to be contracted to provide "gender services" to mainstream institutions. However, the fact that all the gender servicing of mainstream institutions of the last three decades or so has failed to bring about substantive improvements in the status of women vis-à-vis men, only further underlines the need for more critical and conceptually profound approaches than might initially have been apparent. In this meantime, the demand for gender expertise looks set to persist under the various development rubrics—women-in-development, women-and-development, gender and development, gender mainstreaming, and so on. Feminist critics of the whole business of development can be forgiven for suggesting—at times furiously—that all these shifting terms signify is a parasitic relationship of appropriation and neutralization, as women continue to be oppressed and exploited in old and new ways.

What are the intellectual and institutional capacities within the field of gender and/or women's studies (GWS)[13] in African academic institutions that can and are contributing to a radical resistance agenda in African academic institutions?

Feminist intellectuals have generated a large and diverse body of theoretical and conceptual tools, research methodologies and pedagogical innovations and adaptations that are deployed by teachers, trainers, researchers and activists all over the world. They have also produced a substantial body of knowledge, both local and international in its scope, and which displays a rich tapestry of diverse and dynamic political and intellectual trajectories.[14]

Gender and women's studies departments place a premium on their relevance to political and policy considerations, and many of those in the West have internationalized their offerings in an effort to rise to the challenges of globalization. Mohanty describes three variations of this process: the feminist-as-tourist or international consumer, the feminist-as-explorer who is more open-minded but no less voracious a consumer, and finally the feminist solidarity or comparative feminist studies type.[15] Without going into the same level of detail, let me simply note that all these are U.S.-based, and that while we might recognize the "types" and even encounter them all quite frequently, I am more concerned to address the epistemological and practical, day-to-day challenges that face feminist scholars living and working in African contexts.

In this respect it is worth recalling that one of the major contributions of contemporary feminist theory, enriched as it has been by the interventions of feminists based in the global South, is an insistence on being constantly alert to the politics of location and diversities of class, race, culture, religion, and sexuality. Feminist epistemology also seeks to build understanding of the connections between the local and global, between the micro politics of subjectivity and everyday life and the macro politics of global governance and political economy. This reflects a commitment to a certain holism, offering conceptual tools that traverse that various layers of social realities, so challenging and subverting the disciplinary and locational fragmentations that have characterized Western academic traditions. Feminist theorists therefore straddle many intellectual and institutional arenas, in which they face the challenge of keeping global and local levels of analysis in their sights. They must therefore cultivate the navigational and strategic skills required to move between the different levels of analysis, while remaining alert to the fact that these heuristically discernible layers are often interlaced in complicated ways.

In the academic arena, whether one refers to women's studies, gender studies or feminist studies, it is clear that feminist thought has generated a great deal of intellectual ferment across all the disciplines. Feminist studies have often been deeply subversive, overturning pre-existing assumptions, pre-existing histories of knowledge, and transforming pre-existing accounts of human history with rich and interesting herstories that function to complete and to subvert the masculine-dominated canons that went before.

Whatever the local trajectories and conditions that have given rise to feminist activism in African contexts, it is clear that the development of GWS in Africa has been complicated by the global inequalities in knowledge production that favor Western scholarship, as well as by the impact of international development institutions, and their particular gender discourses in African contexts.

Development policy interest in gender has clearly facilitated the growth of gender studies as a field, but there is also evidence to suggest that this has also led to a high level of instrumentalism, seen in the emphasis on policy studies, technical skills and application. The examples discussed below indicate that the developmental interest may also have led to the premature overburdening of a nascent intellectual community that has yet to acquire the institutional capacity to meet the multiple demands for services coming from various quarters. The question of intellectual capacity also arises, particularly given the need for scholars conceptually equipped to do more than passively service disparate policy agendas and to take on higher levels of critical analysis and engagement in the policy arena.

Those calling for gender expertise on the academic front include university administrators, academic colleagues and students, mainstream academic bodies that have yet to develop their own intellectual capacities to engage with gender, and emergent gender studies centers seeking to develop their own skills and capacities. In the practical arena they include governmental officials and policy makers across all the sectors seeking to bring gender into their work, or at least demonstrate that they have attempted to do so. This group includes politicians and activists (many of them women) seeking support in advancing gender agendas in the public arena; international development agencies seeking local informants or consultants; international, national and community-based NGOs and networks. While the exigencies of funding might privilege the use of Western gender consultants in this market, it is also apparent that local gender expertise is also in demand, and might well be more effective given the specific nuance and complexity of gender relations in any particular context. The yawning gap between legal and policy prescriptions on the one hand, and persisting inequality on the other may well have something to do with the prevalence of generic recipes and tools that may often be insensitive to local conditions and sensibilities.

In what follows, I review the institutional capacity for gender and women's studies in Africa, with particular attention to the university departments at Makerere and Cape Town. The purpose of this exercise is to consider the prospects for gender studies realizing its potential as a critical and radical field of work.

Mapping the Terrain[16]

Gender and women's studies has been a growth area over the last two decades. From just a handful of sites in the early 1990s, the field has grown.[17]

A total of thirty universities across the continent responded to the survey, identifying their institutions as sites for teaching and researching gender and women's studies. These universities are Addis Ababa University in Ethiopia; Ahfad University in Sudan; Ahmadu Bello University, Lagos State University, Obafemi Awolowo University, University of Benin, University of Ibadan, University of Nigeria and Usmano Danfodiyo University in Nigeria; Makerere University in Uganda; the Universities of Buea and Yaounde in Cameroon; the University of Cape Coast and the University of Ghana in Ghana; the University of Malawi; the University of Namibia; the University of Sierra Leone; the University of Zambia; the University of Zimbabwe; the Institute for Gender and Women's Studies at the American University in Cairo, Egypt; Rhodes University, the University of Cape Town, Fort Hare University, the University of Durban-Westville, the University of Natal, the University of Pretoria, the University of Stellenbosch, the University of South Africa (UNISA) and the University of the Western Cape in South Africa.

South Africa has the greatest number of gender and women's studies teaching sites, with nine out of the country's twenty-seven universities offering some degree of gender and women's studies teaching. With seven universities out of forty teaching gender and women's studies, Nigeria has the second largest number of gender studies sites on the continent. Ghana and Cameroon identified two universities each serving as gender studies teaching and research sites, while most other countries included in this survey had only one.

The oldest of these are those at the Women's Documentation Centers in the Institute of African Studies at the Universities of Ibadan and Dar es Salaam, while the largest is the Department of Women and Gender Studies at Makerere University.[18]

The number of faculty and students has increased substantially too, and there are signs that gender studies is indeed gaining institutional ground, as the number of sites recognized as full academic departments has also risen during the last few years. The AGI's survey responses indicated that sites for teaching and researching gender and women's studies are structured and administered in a number of different ways. Certain institutions have departments, units, or programs dedicated to gender and women's studies teaching and research, while other institutions have gender interwoven or "mainstreamed" within other, more traditional disciplines or taught courses. Of the thirty institutions, seventeen have dedicated gender teaching and/or research units, programs or departments, while the remaining thirteen institutions offer gender studies as courses or modules within other institutional departments or courses. Dedicated gender programs, units, or departments, for the purpose of this study, are defined as units that specialize in, and have as their core function gender teaching and/or research, with dedicated staff and a dedicated coordinator, director, or chair. The existence of a dedicated gender studies unit can be taken as a superficial indicator of institutional commitment, but for this to be meaningful requires additional investment in infrastructural and highly trained human resources in gender and women's studies.

However, of the dedicated units, only four have full departmental status: the University of Makerere's Department of Women and Gender Studies, the University of Buea's Department of Women's Studies, the University of Cape Town's African Gender Institute, and the University of Zambia's Gender Studies Department.

Only five universities out of 316 on the entire continent offer undergraduate degrees.[19] Twelve of the identified sites teach masters programs (six of these being in South Africa). Doctoral provision is also scarce, with only two sites offering doctoral degrees—the African Gender Institute in Cape Town and Makerere Department of Women and Gender Studies. Despite the demand for places, graduate programs have relied heavily on throughput from strong undergraduate teaching courses, as indicated by the experience of attempts to establish graduate programs in response to demand for gender studies at the universities of Stellenbosch and Witwatersrand in South Africa, both of which have since retracted. The shortage of doctoral programs seems to reflect the dearth of senior-level teaching capacity, as there are hardly any full professors with specialized skills in gender studies, and those willing to supervise doctorates find themselves unable to accommodate the demand. This may change as a few more African women working in gender and women's studies obtain doctorates.[20]

The intellectual content of the teaching varies, but even a cursory survey indicates that the vast majority of them teach in the area of development. Very few teach, or publicly admit to teaching, in more controversial fields, such as sexuality, and those that do place it under the respectable rubric of health or population studies, rather than treating it as a key aspect of gender, or even gender and development. This suggests a degree of intellectual pragmatism, and compliance with administrative rationales and with development servicing, accommodating gender and women's studies only insofar as they present a funding opportunity.[21] Those pouring energy and labor into GWS are often motivated by feminist politics, and pursue a radical and transformative intellectual agenda, perhaps with a degree of discretion. The result is often a conflict of agendas that plays out in invidious and contradictory ways.

Those engaged in teaching point to a number of constraints. Beyond the salient problems of overload and poor remuneration, a major challenge to the development of locally relevant teaching which can support and or develop activist agendas with local women's movements, is posed by the limited availability of locally generated research and publications, and the constrained access to those that do exist.[22]

The existing programs and departments face many challenges. The Department of Women and Gender Studies based at the University of Makerere provides us with a frank and honest appraisal of the achievements and compromises at Africa's largest gender studies department:

> ...the department's experiences in its first decade demonstrate considerable quantitative growth in terms of student numbers, the development of a national and international profile and the expansion of research. This however has occurred alongside a diminishing sense of internal cohesiveness, accountability to the women's movement and engagement with issues of gender transformation in the broader society.[23]

The wider reform effort at Makerere has created a situation in which there are now over 1,000 students enrolled at the

Department, while half of the ten faculty are away pursuing doctoral degrees, now a prerequisite for promotion. The rapidly expanded teaching load has been accompanied by competing demands coming from stakeholders within and outside the university. From within the university have come demands related to gender mainstreaming, notably the work of ensuring that various players are kept aware of the cross-cutting importance of gender, coupled with demands that burden the department with the task of providing all the conceptual and practical resources for implementing "gender mainstreaming." From without have come the competing requests from government for support to the ministry and various women's organizations, and from international donors seeking the training of local development workers. The department tried to respond to these needs by negotiating partnership arrangements with northern institutions. These enabled the department to establish an outreach program in gender training, which set out to achieve the commendable goal of creating "a critical mass of development workers who would work directly with communities to enhance their capacities to meet women's practical needs and to advocate for change where required."

However, despite its popularity with the constituencies for whom it was designed, the gender-training program could not be sustained once donor funding was discontinued.[24]

The AGI, faced with a similar multiplicity of opportunities and requests from within and beyond the campus, has also been subject to shifting donor interests that undermined the initial national program focused on policy analysis, training, and organizational transformation in South Africa, leading to its suspension in 1999. Following this experience, and the appointment of the Chair in Gender Studies, the AGI moved to prioritize the long-term development of critical intellectual capacities and knowledge production, pursued through strong, Africa-focused academic teaching, with an emphasis on feminist methodologies and research. Given minimal core staffing, this necessitated a reduced engagement with policy makers and practitioners. The ensuing years saw the AGI develop a full undergraduate major degree in Gender and Women's Studies, initiating a postgraduate program offering honors, masters, and doctoral degrees in Gender and Transformation, while continuing to host African women scholars, produce research and publications, and run an active website. While struggling to deliver a full academic program designed to produce teachers and researchers, the AGI continued to lobby and strategize with a view to strengthening its institutional capacity within the university. However, the strategy of pursing institutional consolidation through core academic programming has not proved as successful as was originally envisaged, despite the broad institutional expressions of commitment to equity and transformation reflected in university policies.[25]

Ironically, the same recent period of local institutional losses has seen the AGI pursuing its explicitly articulated transformative intellectual agenda on the much broader continental and international fronts that were initially regarded to be a far more ambitious undertaking. 2001 saw the initiation of a continent-wide academic networking and intellectual capacity building program *Strengthening Gender Studies for Africa's Transformation* (GWSAfrica). The broad vision behind this program is that of an African continent enriched by a robust and dynamic intellectual environment which supports African teaching and research in the field of gender and women's studies as a substantive contribution to gender justice. This is pursued through a program of activities to strengthen African teaching and research in gender and women's studies by bringing teachers and researchers based in African universities together in a series of carefully designed intellectual engagements.

The GWSAfrica program was launched at a regional workshop whose participants set out an action plan. This has led to the following activities:

- A regional network of scholars, researchers, and ITC activists has been established.
- A listserv has been established and maintained ongoing discussion and intellectual engagements among network members.
- A project website of teaching and research resources has been established and maintained, with content areas that so far include review essays and bibliographies, policy papers, resources on politics, identity and culture, religion, health, gender-based violence, education, ICTs, land/economics. Special sections are dedicated to student writing and current debates.
- The first continental gender studies journal *Feminist Africa* has been established as an online and hard-copy publication.[26]

• A curriculum strengthening exercise has been carried out and developed supporting resources for those teaching gender and women's studies in African tertiary institutions.

With a small team of project staff, the program has relied on a high level of input and engagement within the primary target community of gender scholars in African institutions and on maintaining close synergy between the different components. So far both have been achieved, as the listserv, website, and journal all support one another, and the intellectual dialogue that has occurred through these systems has informed the curriculum work.

Overall, it is clear that the AGI places great emphasis on working with the community of African feminist scholars to create a supportive intellectual environment and strengthen critical analytical and research capacities. In this sense it differs from conventional academic departments, yet as a strategy it relies on partnership with other centers. To this end the AGI maintains close contact with other sites and envisages further partnerships with these, particularly with regard to gender research.

The emphasis on continental networking draws on the positive experience and connections with the more independent NGO-based organizations and scholarly networks listed above. The AGI attaches particular importance to intellectual transformation, and to this end it seeks to rehabilitate and claim space within academic institutions and insists that universities are legitimate and strategically important sites for feminist work in African contexts. This is particularly challenging given the prevailing academic climate of financial and administrative stringency, in which many African scholars have been habituated to compromise and constraint, and to the ongoing commodification of knowledge. The recent experience of African higher education institutions has posed profound challenges to the emergence of strong, well-rooted, critical perspectives of any kind, including those discussed here, which emanate from feminist though rooted in the unique vantage points offered by diverse African contexts.

Conclusions

I have argued that African GWS has emerged both out of the particular historical and present day challenges facing the continent and African women in particular. The development nexus has complicated the expansion of the field, but at the same time this has enabled it to grow despite the overall deterioration of higher education.

At an institutional level, most GWS sites are under-resourced and understaffed, having been brought about by high levels of voluntarism from a few dedicated women. Their initial establishment has often been facilitated by instrumental interests rather than by any appreciation of what feminist intellectual work entails or offers. This has meant that GWS has been started but often with the institutional support that would guarantee consolidation. Most universities are willing to accept donor funding for such initiatives, while failing to make them sustainable in terms of university budgets and staffing plans. In the long run this will ensure that even the most vibrant and productive sites remain precarious and highly exploitative places to work, relying on dedication and idealism, not to mention the resilience to withstand overarching masculinist institutional cultures that remain intolerant, if not hostile, to feminist ideas and to those identified with them.

The current climate of marketization and cost recovery seems set to intensify the contradictions between politically correct rhetoric, on the one hand, and financial and administrative stringency that underfund social justice concerns, on the other. This is likely to stimulate the development of further critique and analysis, even as it exacerbates the institutional challenges constraining the consolidation of the many sites already in existence. In this context intellectual networking of the type carried out through the regional program to strengthen gender studies assumes heightened intellectual and political importance.

I have argued that the development nexus has been responsible for as many constraints as opportunities, both of which are worth exploring and analyzing. More politicized approaches, such as those offered by feminist theory emerging across the post-colonial capitalist periphery, can and do provide critical conceptual and analytical lenses. These offer valuable tools for demystifying the realities of contemporary Africa and African gender relations by isolating and addressing some of the fallacies currently circulating under the variously named rubrics of women in development, women and development, gender and development, and gender mainstreaming.

Feminist intellectual capacities grounded in contemporary African social and political realities need to be pursued and developed as a means of attaining new levels of activism demanded by the complexities of the times. Existing disciplinary-based academic paradigms largely fail to do justice to the diverse, complex, and changing subjectivities, social arrangements, and material realities that characterize the lives and realities of African women and men. Rather than simplifying, fragmenting, and reducing the many truths out there, we need to embrace new levels of intellectual sophistication and competence, as we move into an era replete with new challenges.

Notes

1. The body of work emerging from African scholars working with feminist and gender theory has grown substantially in recent years. See A. Mama, *Women's Studies and Studies of Women in Africa* (Dakar: CODESRIA, 1996); *Feminist Africa* Issues 1 (2002) and 2 (2003) available at www.gwsafrica.org; D. Lewis, "Review Essay: African Feminist Studies: 1980–2002," African Gender Institute, Cape Town, South Africa (2003) available at www.gwsafrica.org; and *Agenda*, Special Issues on African Feminism 1& 2 (2001).
2. African Gender Institute & AGENDA, *Translating Commitment into Practice* (Durban: AGI and AGENDA, 1999).
3. C. Mohanty, "'Under Western Eyes' Revisited: Feminist Solidarity through Anticapitalist Struggles," *Signs: Journal of Women in Culture and Society*, 28: 1 (2002).
4. Paul T. Zeleza, *Rethinking Africa's Globalization, Volume 1: The Intellectual Challenges* (Trenton, NJ: Africa World Press, 2003).
5. Albeit not to an extent that compares with Asia, which has not suffered the same degree of under-provision.
6. See S. Federici, G. Caffentzis, and O. Alidou, eds., *A Thousand Flowers: Social Struggles Against Structural Adjustment in African Universities* (Trenton, NJ: Africa World Press, 2000) and Zeleza, *Rethinking Africa's Globalization*.
7. M. Diouf and Mamood Mamdani, *Academic Freedom in Africa* (Dakar: CODERSRIA, 1994) and S. Federici *et al.*, *A Thousand Flowers*.
8. Ajayi *et al.*, *The African Experience of Higher Education* (Accra, Ghana: AAU, 1994).

9. *Ibid.*

10. D. Teferra, and P. Altbach, eds., *African Higher Education: An International Reference Handbook* (Bloomington, IN: Indiana University Press, 2003).

11. See *Feminist Africa* 1, 2002.

12. Survey report and Directory available at www.gwsafrica.org.

13. This is a convenient appellation used to address the fact that the naming of departments includes the use of both or either term. Most departments teach feminist theory, methodology, and research, as well as the more institutionally acceptable interest in women and development, gender and development.

14. C. Mohanty, Lourdes Torres and Ann Russo, ed., *Third World Women and the Politics of Feminism* (Indianopolis: Indiana University Press, 1991); M. J. Alexander and C. Mohanty, *Feminist Genealogies, Colonial Legacies and Democratic Futures* (New York: Routledge, 1997), A. Basu, ed., *The Challenge of Local Feminisms* (Boulder: Westview Press, 1997).

15. Mohanty, " 'Under Western Eyes' Revisited." Pp. 518–23.

16. See B. Boswell, "Locating Gender and Women's Studies Teaching and Research Programmes at African Universities: Survey Results (May 2003)," Survey report at www.gwsafrica.org.

17. There are currently over 800 degree-awarding departments and programs in gender and women's studies in the United States.

18. Further details are available at www.gwsafrica.org.

19. These were Makerere Unversity, University of Cape Town, University of Pretoria, University of the Western Cape, and University of Buea.

20. For example, the Universities of Cape Town, Ghana, and Makerere have all seen individual existing faculty return with doctorates in 2003, but restrictions on new hiring continue to pose a constraint and perpetuate the "brain drain."

21. There are parallels with the government structures and project for women that tend to be accommodated where external funding is available, with little allocation in national budgets.

22. See AGI's "Strengthening Gender and Women's Studies in African Contexts," report (2002), available at www.gwsafrica.org.

23. D. Kasente, "Institutionalising Gender Equality in African Universities: the case of Women's and Gender Studies at

Makerere University," *Feminist Africa* no. 1 (2002) available at www.gwsafrica.org.

24. This experience with donor funding has been repeated at many other sites, including a number of continentally based NGO's purposely dedicated to providing gender training.

25. As can be seen in the fact that by 2004 the AGI was more reliant on donor funding that ever. As a result of the constraints within the university, the AGI has temporarily suspended the undergraduate major offered since 1999, in the hope of restarting it with new faculty in 2006, while maintaining the newer and smaller graduate program.

26. The full text of *Feminist Africa*, issues nos. 1–3 is available at www.feministafrica.org.

Contributors

Neville Alexander was imprisoned on Robben Island for his resistance to apartheid. He is currently the Director for the Project for the Study of Alternative Education in South Africa. His most recent book is *An Ordinary Country: Issues in the Transition from Apartheid to Democracy in South Africa*.

Dennis Brutus is Professor Emeritus in Africana Studies at Pittsburgh University in the United States. He graduated at Fort Hare with distinction, studied law on a scholarship at Witwatersrand in Johannesburg, and he was banned under the Suppression of Communism Act in 1961. He was arrested in 1963 in the offices of the South African Olympic Committee and, in January 1964, he was sentenced to eighteen months of hard labor which he spent in part in Robben Island. In 1966, after a year under house-arrest, he was given an exit permit. He is a published poet and has lectured at several universities.

Shereen Essof is a feminist activist, currently based at the African Gender Institute, University of Cape Town. Before that she worked as program coordinator at the Zimbabwe Women's Resource Centre and Network (ZWRCN) in Harare, Zimbabwe. Her current research focuses on women's resistance to capitalism in South Africa. She is an editorial member of the AGI publication *Feminist Africa*.

Jonathan Grossman lectures in the department of Sociology at the University of Cape Town. He is currently working on the development of health and safety training with domestic workers and work around the "new social movements" and the working class. He is active in the UCT Workers Support Committee and the Cape Town Anti-Privatization Forum.

Jonathan D. Jansen is dean of education at the University of Pretoria. He serves on the editorial boards of several international journals that include *Higher Education* and

Qualitative Studies in Education and on international academic councils such as the International Association for the Advancement of Curriculum Studies. He has published in almost every major international journal in education, and his most recent books are *Education Policy Implementation* (2001, with Yusuf Sayed, UCT Press) and *Mergers in Higher Education* (2002, with a team of exceptionally smart doctoral students, UNISA Press).

Fazel Khan began his university career as a worker at the former University of Durban-Westville. He is currently a lecturer in Sociology at the University of KwaZulu-Natal and an executive member of the militant worker-dominated union, the Combined Staff Association.

Mahmood Mamdani has been Director of the Institute of African Studies and Herbert Lehman Professor of Government at Columbia University since he left the University of Cape Town in 1999. His most recent book is *Good Muslim, Bad Muslim*.

Prishani Naidoo is an activist and researcher involved in the Anti-Privatization Forum (APF), Indymedia-SA and Research & Education in Development (Red). She was vice president of the Wits University Students' Representative Council and president of the South African University Students' Representative. She holds an honors degree in Comparative Literature from Wits University.

Andrew Nash is Editorial Director of Monthly Review Press in New York. He taught politics and philosophy for many years at the universities of Stellenbosch and the Western Cape. He has published widely on the history of South African political thought. His book *The Dialectical Tradition in South Africa* will be published by Routledge in 2006.

James Pendlebury is a Johannesburg-based activist who played a central part in the campaign against Wits 2001, in ongoing support work and unionization drives amongst the outsourced workers, and in student and community politics.

Richard Pithouse is a research fellow at the Centre for Civil Society at the University of KwaZulu-Natal in Durban.

Roger Southall is Distinguished Research Fellow in Democracy and Governance, Human Sciences Research Council. He was previously professor of political studies at Rhodes University, and has worked in universities in Uganda, Lesotho, Canada, and the United Kingdom. He has written extensively on South African and African politics, and is a co-editor of the the

HSRC's volumes on *State of the Nation: South Africa 2003-04* and *2004-05*.

Peter Vale is Nelson Mandela Professor of Politics at Rhodes University, Grahamstown. His interests include social theory, security studies and higher education. His most recent book is *Security and Politics in South Africa: The Regional Dimension*.

Lucien van der Walt teaches sociology at the University of the Witwatersrand where he has been active in student politics, in NEHAWU, in the campaign against the Wits 2001 plan, and in the Workers Library and Museum.

Index